To John,

The truth sets us free!

[signature]

27 Sept. 2016

2.7 Soapt

Advance Praise for
For God and Profit

"*For God and Profit* is a formidable book, packed with interesting and regularly unacknowledged and unknown historical information, especially about the contribution of Christian thinking to the development of banking, the rise of the markets and Western prosperity. It is also closely argued with Christian and natural law categories of right and wrong being used to evaluate the economies and financial systems of today and yesterday."

Cardinal George Pell,
Prefect of the Secretariat for the Economy,
Vatican City

"Christians have long been suspicious of the worlds of finance and capital. But Samuel Gregg has produced just the book we need. It is ecumenical, patient in explaining concepts and practices that Christians of all confessions should know, characterized by logic and clear moral analysis, and attentive to the contributions made by Christians throughout history to the development of modern finance systems. At a time when finance not only seems bereft of a moral compass but also to be lurching from crisis to crisis, this is a book sorely needed by Christians today."

Michael Novak, author of
The Spirit of Democratic Capitalism

"Many relationships between people today are based on finance and the exchange of financial value. Often the potential of these relationships and institutions are lost and damaged through harmful action and misguided thought. Both are challenged by Samuel Gregg in this timely, thoughtful, and accessible book. He seeks not only to analyze and critique but to exhort, and his appeal is to reason and the Judeo-Christian tradition. His breadth of scholarship and understanding of contemporary finance make this book a relevant and insightful resource for thinkers and practitioners alike."

Peter S. Heslam, Transforming Business,
University of Cambridge

"In his typically erudite fashion, Samuel Gregg has successfully synthesized an understanding of two topics which are, regretfully, too often seen as being in opposition to one another: God and finance. Grounding his analysis in a narrative which is equal parts modern economics and morality, he leaves the reader thankful for new and at times surprising insights."

Frank J. Hanna III, entrepreneur,
merchant banker and author of
What Your Money Means

For God
and
Profit

"The love of money is the root of all evils," and there are some who, pursuing it, have wandered away from the faith, and so given their souls any number of fatal wounds.

1 Timothy 6:10

But his master answered him, "You wicked and lazy servant! So you knew that I reap where I have not sown and gather where I have not scattered? Well then, you should have deposited my money with the bankers, and on my return I would have recovered my capital with interest."

Matthew 25:26–17

FOR GOD
AND
PROFIT

HOW BANKING AND FINANCE
CAN SERVE THE COMMON GOOD

SAMUEL GREGG

— WITH A FOREWORD BY —
GEORGE CARDINAL PELL

A Crossroad Book

The Crossroad Publishing Company
www.CrossroadPublishing.com
© 2016 by Samuel Gregg

Title by Samuel Gregg
Cover design by Ray Lundgren
Book design by The HK Scriptorium

Library of Congress Cataloging-in-Publication Data
available from the Library of Congress.

ISBN 9780824521882

Books published by The Crossroad Publishing Company may be purchased at special quantity discount rates for classes and institutional use. For information, please e-mail sales@CrossroadPublishing.com.

Contents

Foreword

For God and Profit is a formidable book, packed with interesting and regularly unacknowledged and unknown historical information, especially about the contribution of Christian thinking to the development of banking, the rise of the markets, and Western prosperity. It is also closely argued with Christian and natural law categories of right and wrong being used to evaluate the economies and financial systems of today and yesterday.

For many, the very title, *For God and Profit*, will be provocative. It smacks of political incorrectness. Yet, as Samuel Gregg reminds us, capitalism first developed in the eleventh century, especially in northern Italy and Flanders, and many merchants had that *exact* phrase written in Latin—*Deus enim et proficuum*—in the upper corner of their accounting ledgers. This simply reflected the Christian intellectual framework that shaped thinking and activity in the Middle Ages and was not a cynical expression of materialism. Pursuing profit, taking risks, and creating capital were seen not only as economically useful but also as a way of giving glory to God as people fulfilled the injunction in Genesis to "be fruitful and multiply, fill the earth and subdue it" (1:28).

Western-style capitalism, or what is often called the market economy, is far from perfect. Many remain in poverty. Too many countries have mountains of debts (to the detriment of future generations). Youth unemployment is at catastrophic levels in Spain, Greece, and Italy. The market encourages neither stable marriages nor child bearing. Such a list of ills can be continued.

But today's prosperity remains a stunning achievement that has enabled a better, longer, healthier, and richer life for billions. It is true that no gains are permanent or universal as nothing can be taken for granted and we cannot guarantee that the grandchildren of today's youth, especially if they are from middle-class backgrounds, will be as prosperous as their families are today.

All this is true. But we also have to acknowledge the benefits of the market system, not only in the remarkable economic progress of China, India, and East Asia but also in the United States and the Anglosphere more widely over the past two centuries, and in much of Europe, especially Central and Eastern Europe in more recent decades.

None of this is possible without profit and capital. Moreover, these are more likely when people are God-fearing, know right from wrong, are hard working, honest, and prudent. Widespread corruption damages the economy as it also hardens individual hearts and destroys souls.

Every economy needs a moral framework shared by most of its practitioners. The author of *For God and Profit* is convinced that Christian teaching can contribute much to illuminating the ambiguities and moral challenges in today's economies, provided that Christian commentators, and especially the clergy, have an adequate understanding of the economic activities that they are commending or condemning.

Jesus understood money, as the parable of the talents demonstrates. Matthew recounts (25:26–27) that the man with one talent, condemned by Jesus, did not lose his money. He simply did nothing with it, burying it. Jesus wanted more.

This accurate understanding means that Jesus was speaking from strength when he explains that we cannot choose both God and money (Matt. 6:24; 13:22; 19:22) and makes the notorious warning that it is easier for a camel to pass through the eye of a needle than for a rich man to enter heaven. Greed can be overmastering in every way of life so that it is necessary not to overestimate human goodness and to insist on adequate systems of control and vigilance in capital markets and the financial world more generally.

But to return to the book. The author has a gift of simple explanation for complex concepts and procedures and of unveiling truths long hidden. I did not know, for instance, of the contribution of

Franciscan thinkers (men vowed to material poverty), such as St. Bernadine of Siena, in the thirteen to fifteen centuries to developing an adequate understanding of the changing role of "fertile" money and of the legitimization of charging interest that was not usury and did not exploit the poor. "Triple contracts" are explained. We learn that Christian financial operations dwarfed those of Jews and that in the fourteenth century every bank in Western Europe was either in Italy or a branch of an Italian bank.

Moving closer to our own times, the author underscores the importance of private ownership and monetary stability. He also develops a moral framework, based on the crucial distinction between the fundamental goods, which lie at the heart of human flourishing, and instrumental goods, such as money and capital, which must always be directed to the service of basic goods such as life, knowledge, friendship, work, and the very exercise of reason itself.

The disproportionate ownership of wealth by the top one percent is acknowledged, together with the enormous salaries and bonuses enjoyed by senior financial executives even as they have presided over huge losses during many financial crises, including the Great Recession of 2008. Gregg notes that this raises significant dilemmas. Which firms, he asks, should be bailed out by governments? Do banks have any right to be capitalists in good times and socialists in bad times? Ultimately, the decisions made in the financial world are personal. This means that its practitioners are accountable, even if the speed of transactions has created the "economic herd" and many of the practitioners of finance do not themselves understand clearly what is in their "bundles" or packages of derivatives.

The structures of sin can be real in the world of finance. Hence, the book addresses in detail genuine problems such as odious debt, short-termism, and moral hazard, while urging readers to think more carefully about the nature of practices such as speculation. Yet while Gregg believes that money and finance can be dangerous, liable to spark sinful and even ruthless greed, he also demonstrates that finance is essential to human flourishing, that the poor must never be ignored or forgotten, and that financiers should see their roles as *vocations* and choose and act accordingly.

Gregg does not believe in the "prosperity gospel"—the heresy that holds that faith automatically brings an increase in wealth. Rather, he follows Pope Francis, at least on this point, who has described business "as a noble vocation provided that those engaged in it see themselves challenged by a greater meaning in life," so that they can serve the common good by striving to increase the goods of this world and make them more accessible to all. That is the mission of finance today.

Feast of Sts. Peter and Paul
June 29, 2015

George Cardinal Pell
Prefect
Secretariat for the Economy
Vatican City

1

Introduction

People have to struggle to live and, frequently, to live in an undig-
nified way. One cause of this situation, in my opinion, is in our
relationship with money, and our acceptance of its power over
ourselves and our society. . . . We have created new idols. The wor-
ship of the golden calf of old has found a new and heartless image
in the cult of money and the dictatorship of an economy which is
faceless and lacking any truly humane goal.

Pope Francis, 2013.[1]

With these words spoken to four new ambassadors to the Holy See—
two from countries often labeled as tax havens—a newly elected Pope
Francis expressed the conviction of many Christians that something is
fundamentally awry in the world of finance. On another occasion, Francis stated that Christians who work in financial markets faced particular
temptations that aren't so easily resisted. Then, almost one year after making the remarks cited above, the pope departed from a text of remarks
about the Sacrament of Confirmation to denounce what he described
as the "dramatic social wound" of usury. "When a family doesn't have
enough to eat because it has to pay off loans to usurers," the pope
insisted, his voice rising, "this isn't Christian! It's not human!"[2]

Rather less well known was that the same pope's views of money
were more nuanced than often supposed. In an October 2013 homily, for instance, Francis insisted that neither he nor Christianity was
in the business of demonizing money or those who work in finance.
"Money contributes," he stated, "greatly to many good works for the
development of the human race. The real problem is a distorted use

1

of money, attachment and greed. Hence the Lord's warning: 'Take heed and beware of all covetousness.'"[3] In a speech in 2015, the pope quoted one of the Church Fathers, Basil the Great, to the effect that money is "the devil's dung." Prior to saying these much-reported words, however, Pope Francis carefully noted, in words that went virtually unreported, that money is in fact indispensable if you want to have investment, pay wages, and organize resources.[4]

Christianity has always stressed the potential pitfalls associated with disordered attitudes toward wealth. It has been equally clear that greed, rather than money per se, is the primary stumbling block. Nevertheless, many Christians have been extremely critical—often with good reason—of particular uses of money and capital by individuals, companies, and the state. In the midst of the Great Depression, Pope Pius XI referred to an "accursed internationalism of finance." He even claimed that a "dictatorship is being most forcibly exercised by those who, since they hold the money and completely control it, control credit also and rule the lending of money."[5]

Today one does not have to look far to find similar remarks in the statements of prominent Christians about specific financial practices. In a speech in September 2008 in London to the Institute of Worshipful Company of International Bankers, the Anglican Archbishop of York, John Sentamu, had strong words for those who engaged in short-selling shares. Referring to a spate of short-selling surrounding the British-based banking and insurance company HBOS, the archbishop exclaimed, "To a bystander like me, those who made £190 million deliberately underselling the shares of HBOS, in spite of its very strong capital base, and drove it into the bosom of Lloyds TSB Bank, are clearly bank robbers and asset strippers."[6]

Bank robbers—that's a serious accusation. But one difficulty with the archbishop's statement was that, judging from his speech, it is not clear he understood what short-selling is.

Knowing before Judging

In simple terms, short-selling involves selling a stock that you have borrowed.[7] You may look, for instance, at the stock price of MAG

Enterprises and see that it's currently trading at $1,000 a share. Based on your research and experience, you conclude that the stock is over-priced and likely to decline in price. You consequently decide to borrow 100 shares of that stock through your stockbroker, who purchases the shares and then lends them to you. You are now "short" 100 shares of MAG Enterprises. The short sale is possible only because you borrowed the shares in the first place and you promised to purchase the stock in the future as a way of extinguishing your debt.

One month later, as you anticipated, MAG Enterprises releases poor results for the previous quarter. Stock in MAG Enterprises subsequently plummets to $500 a share. You then choose to close your short position and buy 100 shares of MAG Enterprises on the open market at $500 a share and return them to your stockbroker. In effect, you are buying back the stock at a lower price. Put crudely, this means you only have to pay back half of what you originally owed. The difference (after you've paid your stockbroker a service fee and any dividends earned on the stock during the time of the loan) is your profit.

If, on the other hand, your judgment proves to be wrong and MAG Enterprise's stock rises after one month to $2,000 a share after you borrowed the initial 100 shares (at $1,000 a share) you make a considerable loss. Why? Because you face the prospect of having to pay back twice as much as you initially borrowed.

Short-selling is not for the faint of heart. Nor are the transactions always simple. But looking at the series of exchanges detailed above, the choice to steal or engage in fraud does not manifest itself at any point. Instead, short-selling is about taking risks, and the Christian understanding of justice has always regarded willingness to assume risk as a potential basis for receiving more than those who choose not to take a risk.

There are also several external benefits from short-selling that escape many people's attention. Short-selling has, for example, the broader effect of driving down the price of otherwise overpriced securities. As the English economist and commentator on Christian social ethics Philip Booth notes, short-selling causes "a share price to reflect information quicker than it otherwise would."[8] The pace of price adjustments is thus accelerated, thereby improving the efficiency of financial markets in correctly pricing assets. This is good for everyone.

In other instances, short-selling serves as an early-warning system for fraud—often turning up malfeasance long before regulatory authorities become aware of the problem. It was a hedge fund, for example, whose research first identified problems with Enron's accounting practices, which led the fund to short that stock. That was the first tip-off to the wider world of Enron's inflated revenue reporting.[9] In testimony to the Securities and Exchange Commission, the short-seller concerned pointed out, "Many of the major corporate frauds and bankruptcies of the past quarter century were first exposed by short sellers doing fundamental research: Enron, Tyco, Sunbeam, Boston Chicken, Baldwin United, MicroStrategies, Conseco, ZZZZBest and Crazy Eddie are but a few examples...."[10] Of course, if those involved in short-selling a stock in our fictional MAG Enterprises engaged in spreading rumors and untruths about the company's health in order to drive down the price, that would be wrong. The moral error in such cases, however, isn't short-selling but lying.

My point here is not to belabor the specifics of short-selling. Instead it is to illustrate that a clear understanding of the nature of a given financial practice is necessary before morally assessing it. For many Christians, the work of those involved in finance has always been immersed in a fog of moral ambiguity. One reason for their confusion is their lack of concrete knowledge of what bankers really do and why.

The need to gain such knowledge before rendering moral judgment has been underscored by some of modern Christianity's finest minds. In a response to a question about the 2008 financial crisis during a 2009 meeting with priests, Pope Benedict XVI said,

> I see now how difficult it is to speak with competence on this subject. *If we do not deal competently with the matter, it will not be credible.* On the other hand, it is also necessary to speak with great ethical awareness, created and awakened, so

to speak, by a conscience formed by the Gospel. Hence it is necessary to expose the fundamental errors, the basic mistakes, now being shown up by the collapse of important American banks. . . . We must do so courageously *and concretely, for lofty moralizing does not help if it is not substantiated by knowledge of the facts, which also helps one understand what it is possible to do in practice to gradually change the situation*.[11] [emphasis added]

Benedict was hardly the first Christian to make this point. Similar thoughts were articulated by sixteenth-century theologians engaged in the study of usury. The Spanish Jesuit Luis de Molina (1535–1600) wrote on financial subjects ranging from coinage to taxation, bank deposits, and money exchanges more generally. He went out of his way to consult people actually engaged in these practices, whom he believed would have insights likely to escape a theologian's attention. "The practice of the merchants," he wrote, "makes a better estimation of goods than the scholastic doctors, and the merchants' judgment is rather to be abided by about the value of the goods, especially when they are used in the business they do with one another."[12]

Faith, Morality, and Money

Not only did the bankers of Molina's time understand the workings of money. For the most part, they strove to be faithful Christians. From the beginning of the first forms of capitalism in northern Italy, Flanders, and other parts of medieval Europe from the eleventh century onward, many of the merchants involved in increasingly sophisticated forms of finance wrote inscriptions such as *Deus enim et proficuum* ("For God and Profit") in the upper corners of their accounting ledgers. Others opened their partnership contracts with a formula such as *A nome di Dio e guadangnio* ("In the Name of God and Profit").[13]

One of the most accomplished scholars of this period, the Belgian economic historian Raymond de Roover, insisted that such mottos were neither "an expression of cynicism" nor "a sign of materialism."[14] Instead, these words reflected their authors' conviction that banking and finance were economically useful endeavors, and that in pursuing profit they were in some way giving glory to God by helping to unfold the full potential of the universe he had created.

Molina and the many other Christians who explored these areas throughout history were not searching for greater marketplace efficiencies. Their concern was moral. They analyzed the decisions that people made in finance to see which actions were morally upright and which fell short of the demands of Christian truth.

As important side effects, such studies helped to identify key features of money, clarified how interest worked as a means of calibrating risk, and increased knowledge of the true nature of capital, exploring how it could be used to generate wealth. Nonetheless, Christians were—and must continue to be—primarily concerned with the *morality* of different choices in finance.

Such an approach differs from that of most people studying finance today. Their focus is on seeking to understand and critique contemporary financial practices in order to improve the ability of financial systems to generate *wealth* and realize particular *policy goals*. In doing so these scholars have discovered a great deal about how modern finance functions—knowledge that should be just as helpful for Christians exploring these areas as the findings of scientific research have assisted Christians engaged in medical ethics.

Where the approach of faithful Christians differs from most secular approaches to finance is that Christians cannot accept appeals to expediency or utility maximization as the decisive criterion for making moral decisions. The author of one of the few modern studies of finance from a Christian standpoint, the late Thomas Divine, S.J., stressed this point. The potential for exploitation of borrowers by lenders, Father Divine argued, was dramatically reduced in the conditions of a competitive market for capital precisely because borrowers were no longer at the mercy of one or two lenders.[15] Yet Divine didn't hesitate to affirm, "If the springs of interest are tainted in their source, then no amount of social welfare that interest may promote can avail to purify that source."[16] Divine understood—just as figures such as St. Paul, St. Basil, St. Augustine, St. Thomas Aquinas, and more recently, C.S. Lewis did— that the very stability of orthodox Christian ethics lies in its unambiguous affirmation that there are exceptionless moral absolutes: that is, there are things that may never be done, no matter how much social welfare they may promote.[17]

This doesn't mean that Christians cannot reflect on the foreseeable consequences of a given action. It is entirely legitimate for a Christian to note how short-selling can improve the process of pricing, or to be attentive to inflation's discernible effects on different social groups. There are also many instances in which we may reasonably measure the foreseeable consequences and efficiency of alternative choices. As the moral philosopher John Finnis notes, one such context is a market for those things that may legitimately be exchanged and in which a common denominator (i.e., money) allows appraisals of costs and benefits.[18]

Christians studying finance can't, however, fall into the trap of thinking that it is acceptable to intentionally choose evil in order to realize good. That way of moral choosing and acting was specifically condemned by St. Paul (Rom. 3:8) and the entire orthodox Christian tradition. Moreover, Finnis cautions, making the assessment of calculations the primary points of moral reference is deeply irrational because it assumes the impossible: that humans can know and weigh all the known and unknown consequences of particular actions or rules.[19]

Renewing a Tradition

Though many of us live in religiously pluralist societies in which it can't be assumed that everyone understands Christianity's core beliefs, many people nonetheless want to know what Christians think. It was revealing that, in as secularized a country as Great Britain, the primate of the Anglican Communion, Archbishop Justin Welby, was asked in 2012 to serve on a Parliamentary Commission into Banking Standards. This could be understood as reflecting a dawning recognition that the heavily utilitarian ethics that presently dominates Western societies has failed to produce convincing answers to many of the moral dilemmas facing modern financial systems.

There are, however, four significant impediments to the ability of

Christians to shape today's financial sectors in positive ways. The first is one to which I have already alluded: the widespread unawareness—and, at times, outright ignorance—of finance among Christian clergy of all confessions. In an article in *America* magazine, the Jesuit priest and writer James Martin used some poignant examples to underline just how "at sea" are so many pastors with regard to economics in general and finance in particular:

> Not long after the financial crisis in 2008, one priest confidently told me, "Capitalism is dead." I asked him if he could still go to the corner and buy a hotdog. Yes, he said. "That's capitalism," I said. "It's not dead." A few days later another priest with a Ph.D. asked me, as he read about the financial crisis, "What's a bond?"[20]

From the other end of the finance/Christianity spectrum, it should be said that misunderstandings of Christianity aren't hard to find among those who work in or write about finance. In a *Fortune* article in 2014 about Pope Francis's reforms of the Holy See's finances, one financial commentator asserted, "The paramount duty of the church and its faithful is to aid those in need."[21] Such comments reflect, at best, an inaccurate grasp of what Christianity is about. The Christian church isn't just another NGO, a gaggle of well-meaning do-gooders, or a collection of political activists. Its primary responsibility is to communicate the truth revealed in the person of Jesus Christ to everyone, and to bring all people who accept Christ's message of salvation into the fullness of the Kingdom of God. Everything else in the Christian message—including the promotion of justice in this world (which, by definition, can never be fully realized by sinful human beings)—flows from this.

A second obstacle to Christian reflection on finance is that much of the history of Christians' long involvement in the study of the ethics of money, banking, and finance is relatively unknown not just to the average churchgoer but also to many clergy and theologians. In recent decades, more has been written on this history by deceased and living scholars such as Marjorie Grice-Hutchison, Joseph Schumpeter, Raymond de Roover, John T. Noonan, Odd Langholm, André Azevedo Alves, José Manuel Moreira, Rodney Stark, Diana Wood, and Alejandro Chafuen. Their work, however, remains relatively unknown, even within some Christian circles.

A third hindrance is that relatively few have engaged in the analysis of financial markets or public finance from specifically Christian standpoints. Despite the high volume of discussions of money and finance in the public square, such subjects have received relatively peripheral treatment in modern Christian social ethics. In the twentieth century, most studies of this area were undertaken by a small number of American and German theologians, including the aforementioned Father Divine, but also figures such as Father Bernard Dempsey, S.J., Father Oswald von Nell-Breuning, S.J., and Father Johannes Messner—all long deceased and working in relative isolation from one another. Writing at the end of the 1970s, the Lutheran theologian Wilhelm Kasch lamented the deep gap that had emerged between theology and the study of money.[22] More recent Christian contributions to the study of different aspects of finance have been made by scholars such as Pierre de Lauzun, Jörg Guido Hülsmann, and Paul Dembinski. Yet the number of Christians reflecting on these issues in a sustained manner remains pitifully small.

This leads us to a fourth problem: the fact that much Christian reflection on these matters has not kept pace with finance's increasingly prominent role in modern economic life. This becomes evident when we analyze, for instance, the documents associated with the modern tradition of Catholic social teaching that began with Pope Leo XIII's 1891 social encyclical *Rerum novarum*.

As observed, Pius XI had hard words for the international finance system in his 1931 encyclical *Quadragesimo anno*. Yet his critique hardly went beyond the generalities cited above. This was odd in light of the part played by banking collapses in America and Europe in generating the Great Depression.

Thirty years later, St. John XXIII's encyclical *Mater et magistra* (1961) described "the stability of the purchasing power of money" as "a major consideration in the orderly development of the entire economic system."[23] This, however, is only one aspect of what is encompassed by monetary stability. Monetary stability—understood as the stability of the value of money—also encompasses the relative value of a currency vis-à-vis other currencies (the exchange rate), and the opportunity-cost with respect to amounts of money available in the future (the interest rate). Even the Catholic social encyclical widely regarded as being most positive about market economies, St. John Paul II's *Centesimus annus*, limited itself to observing that a "stable currency" is essential for "steady and healthy economic growth" and constitutes a presupposition for market economic activity.[24]

Since the early 1990s, the financial sectors of developed economies have grown tremendously, as has the role of central banks and monetary policy more generally in influencing the well-being of billions of people. And yet despite acknowledging the fundamental mediating role played by the financial sector in modern economies and noting the benefits and risks associated with what it accurately called "the global capital market," a document on Christian social ethics as comprehensive as the *Compendium of the Social Doctrine of the Church*, published in 2004 by the Pontifical Council for Justice and Peace, devotes just three paragraphs to finance in a text that numbers 583 paragraphs.[25] And while the *Compendium* mentions that it is historically the case that little if any economic growth can take place without financial markets, most of its focus is on the potential for financial markets to do harm.

To its credit, that Pontifical Council is one of the few church organizations that have sought to engage the subject of finance in a relatively comprehensive manner. Following the financial crisis of 2008, for instance, it produced a document that sought to identify some of the causes of the meltdown and possible regulatory measures to be taken as a consequence.[26] Three years later, the Pontifical Council produced a "Note" on the international financial system, entitled *Towards Reforming the International Financial and Monetary Systems in the Context of Global Public Authority*.[27] This repeated many of the observations of the 2008 document but also called for greater top–down regulation on a global level, even mentioning the creation of a global central bank as a serious option worthy of consideration. The Note was subject to widespread and sustained criticisms, many of which came from Christians. It was described, for instance, as insufficiently appreciative of how modern finance actually works at the national and global levels, and as inattentive to the problems associated with excessive regulation and centralization.[28]

In retrospect, however, the Council should be commended for trying to address a subject neglected by most Christians and against a background in which relatively little had recently been written by Christians about money, finance, and banking. Moreover, Christian analysis and criticism of the financial sector and the conduct of central banks were surely merited following the Great Recession of 2008. It was, after all, a crisis partly generated by the financial sector, albeit enabled in many respects by government policies and central bank decisions. Likewise, the debt crisis that brought Argentina to its knees between 1999 and 2001 had a major financial component—a fact that would hardly have been lost on the then-Cardinal-Archbishop of Buenos Aires, Jorge Bergoglio.

So while it's possible to take issue with some of the specific criticisms offered by particular Christians of certain banking and financial practices, there *is* much about modern finance that *does* merit scrutiny from Christians. Consider the following questions:

- Is it just that taxpayers bail out banks and other financial institutions that have manifestly failed?
- Is it ever prudent for a bank to leverage itself at ratios approaching 50 to 1?
- Is it right for central banks to allow mild inflation in an effort to stimulate employment levels, even if it damages the economic well-being of those on fixed incomes?
- How much do those working in the world's stock markets actually know about the companies whose shares they electronically trade by the thousands on any given working day? Is it simply a more sophisticated form of gambling? Or does the process facilitate genuinely wealth-creating efficiencies in the wider economy?
- How much should bankers and other financial sector workers earn by way of salaries and bonuses?
- Should governments be permitted to reduce their debts by devaluing their currencies?

- What should a Christian say about societies in which there is significant recourse by individuals, businesses, and governments to debt, both public and private? When does borrowing become not just economically irresponsible but morally problematic?

These are all reasonable questions. They also indicate just how much modern finance now affects the lives of millions of people. The same questions underscore the complexity of many of the ethical issues associated with finance. Nothing in Christian ethics suggests, for instance, that public or private debt is intrinsically wrong. But how do we determine when a particular burden of debt accumulated by an individual, business, or government has become morally problematic?

In many instances, the rhetoric of some Christians concerning money and contemporary finance is long on indignation but short on knowledge of how, for instance, particular financial instruments work. Are blanket and often uninformed condemnations all that Christianity can offer?

The Way Ahead

This book suggests not. Central to its argument is the claim that Christians have played a long and honorable role in the development of modern finance and banking. It also maintains that finance is an entirely legitimate area in which Christians can participate in good conscience—avoiding actions that destabilize economic life but instead build up the common good. By that we mean conditions that help all to flourish under their own volition. Put simply, a Christian *can* indeed be for God *and* for profit—provided that God comes first and that the profit realized through finance is (1) understood as a means to an end, (2) never seen an end in itself, and (3) used to serve, rather than diminish, what Christians understand as human flourishing.

Finance is unquestionably a sphere of life in which people are subject to particular temptations—just as politics and ordained ministry are callings with their own potential pitfalls that lure people toward

choosing sin. But while the Christian moral life is certainly concerned with not doing evil, finance is far from being an intrinsically
problematic activity. As the French economist and Catholic thinker
Jacques Bichot observes, financial markets are not in themselves
structures of sin: that is, they are not processes and institutions that
are *in themselves* evil.[29] Indeed, the potential to flourish and contribute to the flourishing of others through finance is real.

Our process of analysis, critique, and exhortation begins with
Part I's examination of the long history of Christian reflection
about finance. Here we direct particular attention to how Christians
addressed the issue of usury and, in the process of doing so, helped
turn private finance into an engine that fuels economic growth and
the reduction of poverty. We also consider how Christian minds contributed to the shaping of public finance.

Having established this background, Part II provides a short outline of some of the key principles of a framework for Christians to
think through how finance can promote human freedom, justice, and
the common good. Finally, Part III draws on these principles and the
historical background to articulate Christian responses to some of
the more significant challenges facing modern private finance and
public financial institutions.

Some Caveats

Given the potential scope of any reflection on finance and its role in
today's economies, it is appropriate to outline some caveats concerning our investigation.

The first point to note is that this book is not about money per
se. Clearly, money is a crucial element in any discussion of finance.
There are also important differences between commodity money,
paper money, money certificates, bank money, and credit money.[30]
Money, however, is an enormous subject in its own right. Hence it is
only discussed in these pages when it serves to illustrate wider points
about private finance and financial systems.

A second caveat involves underscoring that this text seeks to be
ecumenical in its sources and reflection. Christians from a range of

churches and ecclesial communities have contributed to discussions ranging from usury to the nature and ends of capital. That said, readers will soon notice that many of the primary sources from which I draw are authored by Roman Catholics. The reason for this is simple. Any survey of the materials authored by Christians on subjects concerning finance soon indicates that the longest and most detailed treatments of these issues have been authored by Catholic scholars, both before and after the Reformation.

Third, this book does not try and provide a definitive answer to every moral dilemma facing Christians working in the financial industry. Certainly there are some questions concerning finance to which the Christian church has very clear answers. Though, as we will see, there are arguments about what constitutes usury, there is no question that usury itself is always wrong. So while Christianity does not have a definitive answer to every single moral question, it does provide sometimes very specific answers to many complex issues and solid principles by which to understand all the others.

Readers won't, however, find in these pages the single definitive Christian answer to the ethical status of practices such as high-frequency trading, credit swaps, shadow banking, flash-trading, derivatives, or quantitative easing. This partly reflects the fact that while Christian ethics is very clear there are certain acts that may never be done because they are by their very nature evil (theft being an obvious example), Christian ethics has also always held that there is often immense room for prudential judgment regarding *how Christians do good* at the level of individuals and communities. On many such matters, governments, communities, and individuals cannot on grounds of reason or Christian revelation identify political or economic arrangements that are uniquely correct. In many instances, they *can* actually identify several options that meet the tests of revelation and right reason, even if some of the options may be incompatible with others.[31] This is the kind of activity of the practical intellect that Aquinas called *determinatio*.[32]

Consider, for instance, the case of taxation. Christian ethics has never disputed that governments may engage in taxation. Yet it has also held, as Alejandro Chafuen summarizes, that any tax law must meet the following requirements:

- *Need*: is there a legitimate necessity for new taxes?
- *Opportunity*: is it the right moment to impose such taxes?
- *Form*: are the proposed taxes proportionate and equitable?
- *Level*: are the proposed taxes moderate or excessive?[33]

Observe that, within these parameters, there is considerable room for Christians to argue among themselves about what constitutes the most optimal taxation arrangements. Likewise, one can say that, provided basic principles of justice are observed, there's no one right Christian answer to, for instance, how those working in finance are compensated. Nor is a single correct answer concerning the optimal size of banks to be found in Christian ethics. To be sure, the sheer size of many large banks raises questions about the capacity of CEOs to know everything they should know about what is happening inside their businesses. It is also reasonable to suggest that the sheer size of some financial institutions makes it easy for bankers to fall into what the former chairman and chief executive of HSBC Group, the Anglican clergyman Lord Green, calls the sin of compartmentalization.[34] Christian ethics in itself, however, does not tell us when a bank has become "too large"—or "too small" for that matter.

The fourth caveat concerns what this book means by "finance." Many institutions and practices are collated together under this broad heading. They range from ratings agencies to day traders who operate out of their homes. Our focus, however, is on two dimensions of modern finance. One is those private investors and investment institutions that compete in financial markets. The other is the state's role vis-à-vis these markets. The reason for this emphasis is simple. As Pierre de Lauzun notes, "these are at the center of the debate."[35]

Finally, a word about audiences. This book is not primarily directed to economic historians, theologians, economists, or specialists in banking and monetary theory. Their work forms an indispens-

able backdrop to this text. To this end, some of the most helpful of
such writings is listed at the end of each chapter. I have, however,
written this book primarily for three groups.

One is clergy of all Christian confessions. Many are asked to com-
ment on finance-related questions by their flocks. Their counsel is
often requested by people working in finance. In the case of Orthodox and Catholic clergy, this extends into the realm of Confession.

Another audience is those Christians working in the private financial sector and public financial institutions, especially those anxious
to bring the insights of Christian faith and morality into their work.

A third and much broader audience is the many Christians who
recognize that there are many problems in today's financial sector
and are wondering how a Christian should try to address them in a
manner consistent with reason and Christian faith.

It is also my hope that this book will be helpful to the Jewish people who work in the financial sector. It goes without saying that many
Jews have suffered, often terribly, at the hands of Christians over the
centuries, and one of the precipitating excuses for the inflicting of
such outrages has been Jewish involvement in finance. Even today,
there is evidence that distrust of finance and financial institutions
correlates highly with parts of Europe in which anti-Semitism was—
and often still is—especially entrenched.[36] Obviously I don't expect
Jews to agree with some of the specifically Christian arguments made
in this text. To the extent, however, that Christian polemics about
issues such as usury have poisoned relations between Jews and Christians, I hope this book provides both audiences with some insight
into constructive ways to think about finance and to relegate myths
from the past to the obscurity they deserve.

Going Backward to Go Forward

One reason why many Christians have historically struggled to
engage finance is that the pace and complexity of economic development often mean there is a considerable time lag between the ability of economists to develop explanations of what's happening in the
economy and the capacity of philosophers and theologians to pro-

vide a moral assessment of new and developing practices. At present, the phenomenon of flash trading is barely understood by some of the best minds in finance. To expect theologians to provide a thoroughgoing moral assessment of this activity hardly seems reasonable.

Another complication concerning Christianity and finance has less to do with issues of intellectual catch-up and more to do with the animus that some Christians have *always* directed against those involved in the business of money and capital more generally. Why is this so? Most Christians, one suspects, would immediately suggest that it has something to do with very public scandals, manifestations of conspicuous consumption, and other expressions of irresponsibility and greed in the financial world. Such factors are certainly part of the answer. A more comprehensive response, however, lies in much of the philosophy, theology, and economics of the pre-Christian and early Christian worlds.

PART I

History

2

Detestable to God and Man

"Once more go back a little to the point,"
I said, "where you state usury offends
The divine goodness, and untie the knot...."

"From art and nature, if you will recall
The opening of Genesis, man is meant
To earn his way and further mankind.

"But still the usurer takes another way:
He scorns nature and her follower, art,
Because he puts his hope in something else."
Dante, Inferno, Canto XI[1]

Widely recognized as one of the high points of Western literature, Dante's *Divine Comedy* reflects some of Christianity's most significant teachings concerning each person's possible fate in the afterlife: specifically, the joy of oneness with Christ in heaven; or, the cleansing of the soul, which some Christians believe occurs in purgatory as a prelude to entry into heaven; or, the eternal separation from God otherwise known as hell.

Noticeable for his prominence in Dante's infernal regions is the usurer. Dante presents usury as so grievous a sin that usurers are confined to the lowest subcircle of hell's seventh circle: an even deeper region than blasphemers and violent murderers.

At some point in their lives, most Christians have heard Paul's words in his First Letter to Timothy concerning the temptations associated with money. This hasn't deterred thousands of believing Christians from working in banking and finance over the centuries. These fields were far from an exclusively Jewish preserve in medieval Europe; some of the most famous international banking families and venture capitalists of the medieval and early-modern period, such as the Medicis of Florence and the Fuggers of Augsburg, were, in fact, Christian and actively involved in the life of the church. After the Reformation and until long into the eighteenth century, European and North American financial markets revolved around Calvinist and Catholic banking families in the Netherlands.

The potential for finance and banking to bring people together— but also to induce catastrophe—has been long understood by Christians. In a book written as much for financiers as for theologians, the Dominican friar Tómas de Mercado (1525–1575) pointed out that a banker "traffics with a whole world and embraces more than the Atlantic, though sometimes he loses his grip and it all comes tumbling down."[2]

Today, many Christians—Evangelicals, Eastern Orthodox, Catholics, Reform, Lutheran, Pentecostal, Anglicans, practicing or non-practicing—work in the world's bourses, banks, and financial institutions. When Pope Francis announced a significant overhaul of the Holy See's financial structures in February 2014, for example, the fact that he was able to appoint seven lay Catholics with established financial credentials to what was called the "Council for the Economy" testified to the extent of Christian involvement in the global economy's financial sector in the twenty-first century.

Nevertheless, profound suspicions concerning those involved in the business of finance are never very difficult to find in contemporary Christian commentary. At one level, these reflect Christianity's blunt warnings that greed can fatally sever a person from life in Christ—potentially forever. In the Scriptures, the writings of Church Fathers, the lives of the saints, and church teachings, such attitudes are regularly associated with excessive attachment to wealth, possessions, and money. Strictly speaking, greed concerns the craving to have something—sex, status, power, material goods—far beyond what a person reasonably needs and what's required by their vocation. Yet Christians generally hear far more about greed and money than they do about, for instance, how greed plays out in politics in the guise of an overweening desire for power.

Scandal Time

The low regard in which many Christians have held the financial sector in recent years owes something to the fact that this has been an area of life with more than its fair share of moral wrongdoing and illegal behavior. From the Savings & Loans crisis that rocked significant sectors of the American financial system in the late 1980s and early 1990s to Bernie Madoff's Ponzi scheme that wrecked the economic well-being of thousands of private individuals, businesses, and foundations, there is no shortage of financial scandals to denounce. Exacerbating these concerns is a widespread perception that banks and other financial institutions receive favorable treatment from governments that isn't as readily accorded to other businesses and companies. Why, many ask, are financial businesses bailed out by governments while other companies are allowed to go bankrupt?

Banks have, of course, been going bankrupt since the time of the ancient Greeks. The vast majority of them have *not* in fact been bailed out. Between 2000 and 2014 alone, the Federal Deposit Insurance Corporation acted as the receiver for approximately 522 failed banks in the United States, most of which were eventually acquired by other banks.[3]

Still, it is hardly surprising that as businesses started to fold, mortgages began to be foreclosed, and thousands of jobs disappeared during the financial crisis of 2008, there was much unhappiness that some of the biggest financial names in the United States—Bank of America, US Bancorp, Citigroup, Discover Financial, Wells Fargo, JP Morgan Chase, Morgan Stanley, PNC Financial, GMAC, Regions Financial, Capital One, American Express, Bank of New York Mellon, State Street Bank—received billions of dollars of assistance from the Federal Government's Troubled Assets Relief Program (TARP). Many of the same institutions also benefited from the Federal Reserve's subsequent forays into quantitative easing through purchasing bank debt, mortgage-backed securities, and U.S.-government debt securities.

Nor has the fact that many prominent Christians and Christian organizations have found themselves mired in financial scandals helped the reputation of finance among Christians. One well-known instance is the *Istituto per le Opere di Religione*—the Institute for the Works of Religion (IOR), otherwise known as the "Vatican Bank." From the late-1970s onward, the IOR was implicated in various scandals, such as the implosion of the Italian financier Michele Sindona's banking empire in 1974, and the bankruptcy of the Banco Ambrosiano in 1982. In the 2010s, several IOR officials were accused of and formally charged with money laundering. Significant reform of the IOR began under Benedict XVI and was continued by Pope Francis. No one, however, can doubt the damage done to the church's reputation by such financial shenanigans.

Another very public case involving prominent Christians concerned the Co-operative Bank, a British retail and commercial bank, whose nonexecutive chairman was an ordained Methodist minister. He was forced to resign in 2013 following the discovery of a hitherto-unexplained £1.5 billion gap in the bank's finances. Less than a decade earlier, the Orthodox Church in Greece had been shaken by a series of major financial embarrassments involving clergy, including one bishop who ended up being jailed after having embezzled €2.5 million in church assets in the 1990s.[4]

Notwithstanding the contribution of these contemporary scandals to many Christians' unfavorable view of finance (not to mention the damage done to Christian credibility), the roots of Christian suspicion concerning money, finance, and banking go much deeper. Curiously enough, some of these are to be found outside the specific history and teaching of Christianity and in the Greek, Roman, and Jewish worlds—cultures that exerted and continue to exert significant influence on Christianity and its views about economic life.

Hellenes, Latins, and Money

Though the Judaism from which the Christian Church emerged was the predominant influence on early Christianity, Christianity first thrived in the Greco-Roman world. The sociologist Rodney Stark has provided considerable evidence to suggest that many of the early conversions to Christianity, perhaps up until as late as the third century C.E., came from heavily Hellenized Jewish communities living outside Judea.[5] Even before the time of Christ, thousands of Hebrews dwelt outside the land of Israel: not just in Mesopotamia and the territories once controlled by the Babylonian and Persian empires, but also throughout the Greek and the then Roman-dominated Mediterranean world.

Greek and Latin philosophy shaped much of the way in which Christian thought expressed itself in the ancient world. Though careful never to reduce Christian faith to philosophy, figures from the apostolic age ranging from St. Paul and St. John the Evangelist to early Church Fathers such as Origen, St. Maximus the Confessor, St. Basil, and St. Augustine of Hippo followed the lead of many Diaspora Jews such as Philo Judaeus of Alexandria (c. 20 B.C.E.–c. 50 C.E.) and readily deployed Hellenistic concepts to explicate and clarify specific theological dogmas and doctrines. As St. Clement of Alexandria (c. 150–c. 225) explained,

> The teaching of the Savior is perfect in itself and has no need of support, because it is the strength and the wisdom of God. Greek philosophy, with its contribution, does not strengthen truth; but, in rendering the attack of sophistry impotent and in disarming those who betray truth and wage war upon it, Greek philosophy is rightly called the hedge and the protective wall around the vineyard.[6]

Moneylending and the charging of interest were everyday features of life in the Greek and Roman worlds in which the first generations of Christians lived. Neither Greek nor Roman law prohibited moneylending or charging interest outright. The utility of these practices made considerable sense in particular segments of these ancient economies, such as the maritime commercial trade that developed throughout the Mediterranean. "The traffic in money," John Keels Ingram writes, "seems to have gone on all through Roman history, and the rate to have fluctuated according to the condition of the market."[7]

In the Greek kingdoms and city-states, pagan temples often loaned money to individuals and the state. Many people deposited their money in the temples because of the inviolability of sacred spaces. There is strong evidence that ledgers of withdrawals and deposits of clients' money were maintained.[8] From what records exist, we know that loans were regularly made to farmers and shipping merchants, with the interest rate generally corresponding to the degree of risk involved.[9] And even this early in history, there were bank failures, most notably during the struggle for dominance between Sparta and Athens throughout the fourth century B.C.E.[10]

Forms of finance and banking were also pervasive in the Roman Empire, and there is no reason to suppose that Christians abstained from using them. Roman law contained extensive regulations governing loans and charging of interest. Many of these provisions dealt with the contracts (known as *mutuum* contracts) governing the lending of goods regarded as fungible (including money), particular nonfungible items lent by one person to another for specific periods of time, and the practice of depositing fungible and nonfungible goods with someone other than their owners.

Roman law also distinguished between usury (*usura* or *foenus*) and interest (*id quod interest*). The former concerned payments for the use of money. As Divine notes, it covered any "charge made for the loan of any good that fell within the class of what was called *mutuum*, i.e., a loan of consumption or 'fungible' good."[11] Interest, by contrast, was the recompense for any loss or damage by creditors that followed from a debtor's failure to repay the loan according to the date stated in the contract.[12]

Despite, however, the prevalence and significant degree of institutionalization of rudimentary forms of finance throughout Greco-Roman societies, most Greek and Latin philosophers and citizens maintained a low view of commerce, especially anything to do with moneylending per se. The Greek disdain for manual labor and commerce meant that banking activities in the form of moneychanging, moneylending, and maintaining deposits were generally undertaken by the metic class (those who were neither citizens nor slaves) or foreigners.[13]

In Plato's case, much of his dislike of moneylending flowed from his conviction that it was impossible for happiness and the possession of wealth to go hand in hand. In his *Republic*, Plato portrayed usury as irredeemably flawed and a means by which rulers could corrupt the state:

> Since its rulers owe their offices to their wealth, they are not willing to prohibit by law the prodigals who arise among the youth from spending and wasting their substance. Their object is, by lending money on the property of such men, and buying it in, to become still richer and more esteemed . . . these money-makers with down-bent heads, pretending not even to see them, but inserting the sting of their money into any of the remainder who do not resist, and harvesting from them in interest as it were a manifold progeny of the parent sum . . . and so they make drone and pauper to abound in the state.[14]

Aristotle did not embrace what can only be described as Plato's protocommunist view of property. He also distinguished between money as a convention that helped us to measure value and money as something of intrinsic value (because it was made of a precious metal).[15] Despite these differences with Plato, however, Aristotle was equally condemnatory of the money trade. To some extent, this reflected Aristotle's belief that commerce encouraged materialism and distracted citizens from the pursuit of higher values.[16] But there were three other reasons for Aristotle's particular animus against markets for money.

The first was the manner in which Aristotle believed that usury discouraged the virtues of liberality and generosity toward others, especially the poor. Second, Aristotle thought moneylending encouraged people "to make gain in improper ways."[17] By this, Aristotle meant that the charging of interest was an unnatural use of money and thus a violation of justice. The natural purpose of money, in Aristotle's view, was to facilitate exchange. To "breed" money from money by charging interest was thus unnatural.[18] Third, Aristotle argued that moneylending distorted economic activity by shifting people's focus away from satisfaction of wants and toward an endless quest for the unlimited accumulation of wealth.

Roman thinkers such as Cicero, Cato, and Seneca were just as censorious of moneylending and charging interest as the Greeks. Following Aristotle, Seneca condemned charging interest because money, he held, was barren by nature. He also maintained that charging interest effectively amounted to the sale of time. Since life itself was measured in time, Seneca argued, charging interest was as wrongful as murder.[19] Cato's condemnation of moneylending flowed from his conviction that it was a dishonorable activity—a connotation that meant a great deal in the deeply honor-conscious Roman world in which certain activities were seen as simply beneath those who were Roman citizens.[20]

Though Christianity first flourished in the culture created by Rome and Greece, it also rejected many aspects of the Greco-Roman world. In the realm of morality, for instance, Christianity specifically condemned widely accepted pagan practices such as abortion, contraception, and infanticide. Christianity also bestowed on women a dignity unprecedented outside the Jewish world, not least because of its prohibition of divorce and remarriage.

Nevertheless, it would have been strange if Greek and Roman culture did not exert some influence on Christianity. As noted, many early Christians valued specific aspects of Greek and Roman thought. In the case of money, however, Roman and Greek views of usury, interest, and moneylending coincided with certain facets of Judaism's perspective on such matters.

Israelites and the Poor

In an article in 1966, one of the most prolific scholars on the usury question, John T. Noonan, claimed that all return on a loan was condemned "absolutely, unequivocally, without exception" by the Old and the New Testaments.[21] Yet, as the equally learned Father Thomas Divine illustrated at the time, Noonan's rather dramatic claim was not correct.[22]

The Hebrew Scriptures are replete with warnings about money. In particular instances, it also condemns charging interest. The book of Ezekiel, for instance, identifies usury and the taking of interest as an "appalling crime," placing it in the same category as adultery, stealing from the poor, idol worship, and theft. Anyone who engages in such a practice, the prophet promises, "shall certainly not live" (Ezek. 18:10–13).

Other scriptural verses, however, focus on those who profit from the needs of the indigent (especially fellow Israelites but also, in some instances, the non-Jew living peacefully in the land of Israel), rather than acting mercifully and helping them with no expectation of return. This is regarded as akin to extortion (Deut. 15:7–9; Eccles. 29:1–5). But it leaves open the question of the legitimacy of lending to those people who are *not* poor.

Some scriptural texts warn against lending *any* type of commodity to any member of the Hebrew people whatsoever, but permit lending to non-Jews (Deut. 23:19–21). The significance of these particular verses lies in the fact that they provided later generations of Jews with a scriptural basis for engaging in moneylending to gentiles, first throughout the Roman Empire and then the post-Roman world of Christendom. It hardly needs to be stated that some of the worst expressions of Christian anti-Semitism over the centuries have referenced Jewish involvement in moneylending. Many cases of violence against Jewish communities in medieval Europe had much to do with some Christians' desire to destroy the records of the debts that they owed to Jewish moneylenders. Often they targeted the lives of the moneylenders themselves.[23]

The point, however, is that the Hebrews did not regard the condemnation of moneylending as absolute. As the Jesuit social ethicist Rodger Charles notes, moneylending was in fact widespread among the ancient Israelites. Lenders, Charles adds, were seen as entitled to the eventual return of their loan, though it was seen as morally better to forgo the repayment if the lender could afford to do so.[24]

Here we should note that most Hebrew scriptural verses on the subject associate charging interest with the negative social impact on one's fellow Israelites and the failure to help those in need. Most usury verses refer, for instance, to wealthy people lending money to the poor and exploiting those in poverty instead of acting benevolently toward them. Many of the scriptural directives concerning the jubilee cancellation of debts were focused on rectifying the situation of Israelites in poverty—even if such cancellations seem not to have occurred in practice.[25]

All this reflects an economy and economic life heavily based on the possession of land and agriculture. In the preexilic kingdoms of Israel and Judah, foreign trade and large-scale commerce seem to have been undertaken by nearby Phoenician traders.[26] Most loans by Israelites to other Israelites tended to be made for either consumption or agricultural purposes. Given the unreliability of crops in a land of small farmers lacking the techniques and technologies that we take for granted today, exploitation of the rural poor through moneylending was a real possibility. The high interest rates invariably attached to these types of loans (because of the significant default risk), combined with the sheer number of people working in agriculture, only served to increase the opprobrium attached by many Israelites to moneylending as a profession and practice.

Having looked at all the scriptural evidence from the Hebrew scriptures and associated historical background, Father Divine concluded several decades ago:

> The only conclusions that we can draw from the texts of the Old Testament are that: 1) Usury was prohibited in the case of loans made to the poor. 2) The taking of interest was permitted in the case of loans to "strangers," i.e., the Egyptians, Babylonians, Phoenicians, etc. with whom they were engaged in trade. 3) Avarice and greed which resulted in amassing riches by oppressing the poor was condemned, while generosity and charity in lending without interest to needy brethren was highly praised.[27]

That hardly amounts to an absolute, unequivocal, and exceptionless condemnation of either moneylending or charging interest.

Premedieval Christianity, Money, and Interest

Traces of many of the aforementioned concerns about moneylending and charging interest manifest themselves in early Christian treatments of this subject. However, it is not true that the New Testament unequivocally condemns charging interest.[28]

The New Testament's strictures against the dangers associated with disordered attitudes toward material wealth hardly need repeating. Christ's clear warning that one cannot serve both God and money (Matt. 6:24; 13:22; 19:22) is echoed by Paul's emphasis on the folly of wealthy people putting their hopes in one's possessions (1 Tim. 6:17). Christianity didn't, however, teach that those who possessed wealth were somehow beyond salvation. Nor was anyone guaranteed a place in heaven by virtue of living an earthly life of material poverty.

Concerning the specific subject of usury, the New Testament says relatively little. The hard words directed by the master toward the lazy cowardly servant in the parable of the talents (Matt. 25:27; Luke 19:23) imply neither condemnation nor approval of the practice of lending at interest. Having studied these scriptural verses, Divine concludes, "If any conclusions are to be drawn as to the attitude of Christ implied in this parable, we cannot see how they can be other than favorable to the practice of lending at interest for commercial purposes. For we would not expect our Lord to compare Himself to a master who would exact of His Servants conduct that is morally reprehensible."[29]

Even those verses in Luke's Gospel—specifically Luke 6:34–35—in which Christ speaks negatively of lending in the hope of return don't lend themselves immediately to a condemnation of moneylending per se. Certainly some Christian authorities would treat these sentences as a major source for their condemnations of usury. Pope Urban III, for instance, used this verse to specify that usury was a sin of *intention*: that of expecting to receive back more than one gives.[30] Nonetheless, the focus of the relatively few New Testament statements about moneylending seems less concerned with charging interest in itself. Rather they echo the Hebrew scriptures' emphasis on the need to be generous toward, rather than exploitative of, the poor.

The next source of Christian teaching to check, after the Bible itself, is the Church Fathers—those commentators noted for their orthodoxy, learning, holiness of life, and authority, who "unpacked" between the first and eighth centuries the teaching of the Gospels and the tradition imparted by the apostolic generation. Their statements on usury largely amount to a reiteration of scriptural pronouncements. Clement of Alexandria underlines those Hebrew scriptural verses that stress not charging interest to those who are our neighbors.[31] Other Church Fathers discuss usury in the context of the exploitation of the poor. This is linked with the Christian emphasis on mercy. In his famous homily on Psalm 14, "Against Usury," for instance, St. Basil the Great (who came from a wealthy family), states,

> For in truth it is the last pitch of inhumanity that one man, in need of the bare necessities of life, should be compelled to borrow, and another, not satisfied with the principal, should seek to make gain and profit for himself out of the calamities of the poor.[32]

One of the early Latin Church Fathers, Lactantius (c. 240–c. 320), an advisor to Emperor Constantine, underscores the injustice of receiving back more than one has given in a loan, though within the context, it should be noted, of preying on those in poverty.[33] The same understanding of usury is articulated in St. Jerome's commentary on Ezekiel. Again, however, it rests on the supposition of a wealthy person loaning money to the poor.[34]

As noted by the Anglican historian of the early church, Henry Chadwick, "it does not appear that objection was seriously taken to loan capital for commerce and there is considerable evidence of the clergy providing a banking service for their congregations."[35] In his *History of the Franks*, for instance, St. Gregory of Tours (538–594) refers, without any condemnation, to a bishop who asked the monarch for a loan of money on behalf of a group of merchants which the bishop promised to return with "legitimate usury" [*legitimis usuries*].[36]

Alongside these commentaries, however, we must consider the ways in which the Christian church itself spoke formally on this subject. Usury was not mentioned by the very first church council, the Council of Jerusalem (c. 50). Nor does it figure in the *Didachē*, a late-first- or early-second-century text of Christian moral instruction. One of the canons of the general Council of Nicaea (325) stressed the impermissibility of clergy engaging in moneylending on the basis of Psalm 14. Other early church councils, ranging from the provincial Council of Elvira (c. 306) to the first Council of Carthage (345), likewise prohibited clerics from practicing usury—the prescribed punishment being excommunication—and expressed strong disapproval of laypeople engaging in moneylending . In an epistle to several Italian bishops, *Ut nobis gratulationem* (443), Pope St. Leo the Great stated that those laypeople who engaged in usury were guilty of shameful gain, and he too expressly forbade clerics from the practice.[37]

By the eighth and ninth centuries, synods and provincial church councils such as Aix-la-Chapelle (789), Paris (829), and Pavia (850) had formally prohibited laypeople from engaging in usury.[38] Certainly these were not dogmatic definitions. As observed by the French medievalist Jules Favre with regard to the Council of Paris, "The council is merely an echo of the universal complaints against the usury of the period, where in utter disregard for any consideration of humanity, the poor are reduced to starvation and misery."[39]

Nonetheless, opposition to and prohibition of usury were beginning to acquire definitive expression in ecclesiastical and civil law during this point in history. By the end of the first millennium, the law of the Holy Roman Empire sought to ban not just clerics but also laity from the practice. During the same period, many bishops began punishing clerical usurers within their dioceses.[40]

In the eastern Roman Empire, a somewhat different economic pattern prevailed. The world of Byzantium remained economically ahead of the Catholic West until at least the tenth century.[41] Located at the epicenter of trade routes between East, West, North, and South, commerce remained much more extensive throughout Byzantium than in the West, perhaps because of the greater number of easily accessible coastal towns and cities. Likewise, the population decline experienced in the West was not initially replicated to the same extent in the Christian East. A more formalized banking system was maintained in place for a much longer period of time throughout the Byzantine Empire, perhaps because of the imperial government's resistance to currency debasements until the tenth century. Despite being frowned upon by the church, the charging of interest remained widespread, particularly with regard to merchant shipping. Nonetheless, Byzantine legal codes became stricter over time in regulating what rates could be charged, especially for farmers.[42]

There are, however, some important qualifications to be made about this general picture. In the first place, there appears to have been no significant effort by the church to define what constitutes a loan, let alone the specific characteristics of different types of loans. Second, while usury was certainly seen as a serious sin, the question of its relationship to justice seems primarily to do with abuse of the poor. In premedieval Christian writings and teachings, it is harder to find any parallels to Aristotle's objections to usury as a perversion of the nature of money. These factors underscore the importance of *context*, both economic and intellectual, in understanding the Christian approach to money and finance—and not just in the first millennium but also in our own time.

Zero-Sum Economies, Zero-Sum Economics

Perhaps one of the most important points to grasp with regard to the views taken of finance during the time periods surveyed above is that the general economic environment was not at all conducive to the creation of wealth. These were not economies in which steady growth was occurring on a widespread and more or less permanent basis. Economic conditions for virtually all of these periods remained dominated by various combinations of subsistence farming, slavery, and the economics of plunder and expropriation via levies, tribute, and taxes paid by the conquered to the conquerors.

Until the coming of the *Pax Romana*, the land of Israel was surrounded by countries constantly at war with one another. Under

Roman rule, most of the population of Judea and Galilee remained poor and focused on agriculture. Great wealth disparities existed between them and the small elite of civil and religious rulers, some of whom collaborated with the Roman authorities. Much of the day-laborer rural population was often deeply in debt to the landowners.[43]

Things were not much different in the wider Roman Empire. Roman law, legions, public works and administration brought civil peace to hitherto unstable parts of the world. But the fact remained that the empire had been primarily constructed by the sword, and the economy remained overwhelmingly agricultural. This is one reason why most taxation throughout the empire came from assessments of farm stock and land.

Roman economic life was in many respects unapologetically exploitative. Most labor was carried out by millions of slaves. Rome itself relied on large imports of grain supervised by the state authorities anxious to keep the Roman plebian class happy.[44] Nor did demands for the upkeep of the Roman administration and legions abate. Taxes were constantly being raised while the economy's capacity to produce even subsistence-level growth steadily decreased. One way in which the empire tried to deal with shortfalls was through currency depreciation. This in turn bred inflation. As Charles observes, the failure to maintain "a sound currency was particularly damaging, so crucial was it to trading confidence."[45]

The Roman state's inability to manage its public finances worsened the overall situation. Like most of the Greek states' rulers, the empire's administrators were apt to use public finances to curry favor. At one point, something like 200,000 people in Rome were receiving distributions of wheat from the state free of charge.[46] Eventually, crumbling finances and successive currency debasements forced the Emperor Diocletian (284–305)—a talented administrator and one of Christianity's greatest persecutors—to develop what amounted to the world's first annual budget. Though this helped restore fiscal order and some monetary stability, it wasn't enough to prevent the empire's steady decline.[47] Adding to the overall pattern of economic stagnation was the fact that the birthrate throughout the empire had begun declining by the time of Christ—a trend exacerbated by the widespread practice of infanticide and abortion among Greeks and Romans.

In the centuries leading up to the Middle Ages, agriculture continued to dominate economic life, albeit increasingly regulated by feudal structures and expectations. The development of self-contained economic units based on feudal principles led to even further declines in trade. At one point in the history of post-Roman Britain, commerce had deteriorated to the extent that, for a two-hundred-year period between the fifth and seventh centuries, the use of coinage virtually disappeared and a barter economy emerged.[48]

But even more fundamentally, the inability to develop sustained patterns and institutions of wealth creation was a problem of *ideas* and a failure of imagination. Part of this involved the often-negative view of work taken by Greek and Roman elites. Creating wealth was never going to be a priority for those who regarded politics and war as infinitely superior occupations to that of a merchant.

Judaism and then Christianity extolled work. But some Church Fathers articulated a less-than-favorable view of commerce. Pope Leo I, for instance, indicated that it was very hard for sellers and buyers in an exchange to remain free of sin. St. Jerome even went so far as to claim that fraud and trade were one and the same![49]

The periods mentioned above were also marked by the *absence* of economics—in the sense that this discipline is understood today. The "hows" of wealth creation went relatively unexplored by the Hebrew prophets, Greek philosophers, Roman lawyers, the apostolic generation of Christians, and the Church Fathers. Though there is a type of economic thought present in Aristotle,[50] the prevailing wisdom tended to be that one person could only become wealthy at another's expense because the world's total sum of wealth was more or less fixed.

The same way of thinking suggests that if there is not enough to go around, it must be because some people have more than they need and are refusing to share. Further clouding people's perspective was an absence of understanding how capital formation and investment facilitated the division of labor and therefore an increase in the sum total of wealth. Missing also was the recognition that money could be created in the present not simply out of savings but also from the expectation of future profits and earnings.

This combination of political, demographic, institutional, and intellectual factors meant that, over time, more and more people in these predominantly agricultural societies sank into poverty during Christianity's first nine hundred years. Borrowing money throughout these centuries was thus largely for purposes of consumption—in order, for example, to survive crop failures. The opportunities for exploitation by moneylenders willing to take advantage of the numerous cases of necessity were thus magnified. People became trapped in escalating spirals of interest payments. Interest rates were also extremely high, mainly because of the risk undertaken by the lender. Favre notes, for instance, that the level of interest rates prevailing by the ninth century "surpasses anything that one could imagine of infamy and extortion—100, 200 and even 300 percent. For a bushel of wheat or a measure of wine, the lenders demanded three or four in return at the time of harvest."[51]

A New Economic World

Given this context, it's not surprising that the focus of much Christian thinking about economic life remained firmly on preventing, resolving, and punishing injustices in economic life. It also helps explain the church's increasingly hard line against moneylending throughout society and the civil power's enactment of laws that went beyond regulating charging interest toward trying to abolish it altogether.

Christianity's position vis-à-vis moneylending and finance, however, cannot be completely explained by the character of economic life of the time or the absence of a sophisticated economic science. For the most part, Christians who discussed issues such as charging interest primarily focused on the morality of *acts* of moneylending, particularly the *intention* to act against mercy and charity toward one's brothers and sisters in Christ, especially those enduring material poverty. In an economically challenged world, where poverty was the norm, it was very difficult to understand the act of lending money and charging interest as being driven by anything but the intention to exploit those in need.

Yet within two hundred years of the tightening and widening of prohibitions in civil and canon law concerning usury, the subject of finance became a major area for discussion and development of thought within the Christian world. This owed something to Western Christian thinkers taking a deeper interest in what figures such as Aristotle had said on this subject in the wake of a steady influx of ancient Greek thought from the Orthodox East.[52] It also reflected, however, a stunning economic event: the emergence of the world's first capitalist economies. And though the Christian condemnation of usury remained, the study of this subject and the subsequent deepening of insight not only resulted in Christians making major contributions to the development of ideas that continue to shape finance today; it also opened up the possibility of positive assessments of finance by Christians.

Further Reading

Bang, Peter Fibiger. *The Roman Bazaar: A Comparative Study of Trade and Markets in a Tributary Empire*. Cambridge: Cambridge University Press, 2008.

Divine, Thomas, S.J. *Interest: An Historical and Analytical Study in Economics and Modern Ethics*. Milwaukee: Marquette University Press, 1959.

Finley, M. I. *The Ancient Economy*. Oakland, CA: University of California Press, 1973.

Stark, Rodney. *The Rise of Christianity: A Sociologist Reconsiders History*. San Francisco: Harper, 1996.

Thornton, James. *Wealth and Poverty in the Teaching of the Church Fathers*. Berkeley, CA: St. John Chrysostom Press, 1993.

Wheeler, Sondra Ely. *Wealth as Peril and Obligation: The New Testament on Possessions*. Grand Rapids, MI: Wm. B. Eerdmans Publishing, 1995.

3

Financial Revolution

Christianity and
the Rise of Capital

*Money has not only the character of money, but it has beyond this
a productive character which we commonly call capital.*[1]

St. Bernardine of Siena

Given that he was a member of the famously ascetic Franciscan order
with his own reputation for detachment from worldly things, Bernardine of Siena (1380–1444) was remarkably insightful about money.
Most people are understandably surprised to learn that some of the
important intellectual developments that first enabled finance to
become an engine of growth were made by men who had, for the most
part, freely taken vows of poverty. Almost a century before Bernardine,
another Franciscan, Peter Olivi (1248–1298), had written the following
in his *De contractibus usurariis*:

> For since money or property which is directly managed by its
> owner is put to work for a certain probable gain, it not only
> has the simple quality of money or goods, but, even beyond
> that, a certain seminal quality of generating profit, which we
> commonly call capital ... and therefore not only does the simple value of the object have to be returned, but also an added
> value.[2]

Like all medieval clergy, Olivi and Bernardine fiercely opposed usury. "Usury," Bernardine wrote, "concentrates the money of the community in the hands of a few, just as if all the blood in a man's body ran to his heart and left his other organs depleted."[3] Yet the same Bernardine also invested time in explaining why it was legitimate for creditors to charge interest on loans to compensate themselves for relinquishing the opportunity to invest their money elsewhere. In such circumstances, the lender had a right to be compensated for what amounted to foregone profits. "What," Bernardine maintained, "in the firm purpose of its owner is ordained to some probable profit has not only the character of mere money or a mere thing, but also beyond this, a certain seminal character of something profitable, which we commonly call *capital*."[4] This title, known as *lucrum cessans* (profits given up, or what we today might call the *opportunity cost* of liquid funds) reflected the insight that money was not always sterile and could become productive: money could turn into capital.

Franciscans didn't limit themselves to writing about such issues. From the fourteenth century onward, they sought to help the needy gain access to credit in the form of loan companies.[5] More popularly known as *montes pietatis,* the first of these lending institutions was established by Franciscans and initially funded by donations from wealthy Christians. They lent money to relatively poor people unable to access loans from established moneylenders. Borrowers would provide the *montes* with small items of value as a form of security for the loan's repayment.

Controversy arose, however, when the *montes* began charging interest, ranging between 4 and 12 percent. One of their strongest boosters—another Franciscan who spent much of his time decrying moneylending in general and (alas) Jewish moneylenders in particular,[6] Blessed Bernardine of Feltre (1439–1494)—insisted that some charging of interest by such institutions was essential if they were to become self-sustaining.[7] Eventually this became the norm for all Franciscan-established *montes*. Not surprisingly, they were eventually accused of engaging in usury.

The *montes* and their practices of charging interest were, however, vindicated, first by Pope Paul II in 1467 when he approved the original *mons* in Perugia,[8] and then by Pope Leo X in 1515 in the papal bull *Inter multiplicis*.[9] Hundreds of *montes* subsequently emerged throughout Italy, France, Austria, Germany, Flanders, and Spain. One of the earliest, the Monte dei Paschi di Siena, was founded in 1472. It still exists today and is Italy's third largest bank, employing thousands of people around the world.[10]

Despite papal approval, accusations of usury against the *montes* didn't disappear. This produced defenses of their charging of interest by scholastic thinkers, such as the sixteenth-century Dominican Martin de Azpilcueta (1491–1586). He argued that the interest was, strictly speaking, not a direct payment for the loan but a charge for administering the loan.[11]

Many people today look at the way in which Christian thinkers reacted to these developments throughout the medieval and early modern period with some cynicism. More than one person has suggested it amounted to Christians engaging in torturous semantics to help Christianity accommodate itself to widespread economic changes as the world's first forms of capitalism began taking root in medieval Europe.

To reduce such intellectual development to a crass adjustment to circumstances would be a mistake. Certainly context is important. But it's also true that an environment of immense economic change stimulated many Christian scholars from the eleventh century onward to *rethink* the nature of money. Over time, they developed a series of important insights and clarifications, the most significant being a clear distinction between usury and legitimate forms of moneylending.

These writers did not approach these issues as "economists." They addressed these questions in the context of moral theology and law. The sophistication of their analyses was such, however, that as noted a modern economist and historian of economics as Joseph Schumpeter (who famously coined the phrase "creative destruction") could affirm that "we behold an embryonic *Wealth of Nations*" in scholastic thought.[12]

From Stagnation to Growth

Given the hardening of canon law and civil law's strictures against usury in the period preceding the Middle Ages, it's remarkable that subjects such as money, capital, interest, and loans occupied so much attention from Christians over subsequent centuries. This was partly driven by ongoing theological investigations of usury. The intensity of that analysis, however, owed something to the fact that Western Europe underwent during the same period what the medieval historian Robert Lopez has called a Commercial Revolution.

As Lopez describes it, "Catholic Europe moved from stagnation at the lowest level to a social and economic mobility full of dangers but open to hope" toward the end of the tenth century.[13] The vicious circle of low production, small consumption, and population decline that had followed the Roman Empire's slow-motion implosion was broken by what another medievalist calls a "spectacular transformation" in Western economic life.[14] Population growth and technological innovations (such as the application of machine power to agriculture and manufacturing) led to more intensive farming. This produced more products, industry, trade, and, most importantly, surplus capital: capital that could be mobilized for investment and that could help move society beyond subsistence economies.

Accompanying these economic changes was the rise of urban towns. The predominant mode of life remained agricultural for most people, and medieval European society continued to be deeply stratified. Nevertheless, upward economic mobility became a distinct possibility for more people, and such movement was primarily found in cities. Thriving business communities emerged in northern Italy, Flanders, parts of France, and southern England. Alongside this emerged inter-European trade, a transnational division of labor, and a new class of entrepreneurs who coordinated business organizations and engaged in what we today call marketing.[15]

These and other changes did not simply amount to a type of protocapitalism. It was, as Randall Collins writes, "a version of the developed characteristics of capitalism itself."[16] The growth of commerce, urban living, and business went hand in hand with the spread of commercial mindsets, values, and priorities throughout Europe.[17]

Finance and the New Economy

A crucial element driving many of these developments was the refinement of several conceptual tools that gradually assumed legal and economic form. To this extent, the Commercial Revolution was as much a mind-driven change as a reflection of demographic and productivity trends.

A good illustration was the proliferation of legal instruments such as partnership contracts. These reduced costs and smoothed the process of exchange. By the thirteenth century, single-entry bookkeeping had emerged—a critical tool by which people were able to assess more accurately a given economic venture's true costs. As trade expanded, Italian merchants developed double-entry bookkeeping to distinguish cash receipts from cash payments. This helped formalize the rule that there should never be a debit without a corresponding credit.[18] Important accounting concepts such as the depreciation of goods and the distinction between revenue and capital did not take long to emerge.[19]

As the Commercial Revolution unfolded, measuring, calculating, and estimating became part of everyday life, especially through the means by which one could weigh such things: money. This was further spurred by the application of mathematics to financial calculations as early as the twelfth century. The way forward had been smoothed by the replacement of Roman numerals by the less cumbersome Arabic numerical system and a corresponding increased use of the abacus.

In his 1202 book *Liber abaci*, Leonardo of Pisa (1170–1240) applied mathematics to questions such as price determination in light of increasingly complex currency exchanges or the just distribution of profits from an enterprise to which various people have contributed different amounts of investments at varying times in disparate currencies. He also helped pioneer the calculation of an investment's future value, the difference between quarterly and annual compound interest, and the determination of profits from a sequence of banking deposits made over extended time periods.[20]

Alongside these tools emerged a number of financial instruments that helped merchants manage risk. Until the end of the eleventh century, European merchants lived rather itinerant lives. Their travels, whether on sea or land, were dangerous. Merchants began, however, to realize that their risks could be minimized by traveling together and forming partnerships. They devised several financial tools that enabled them to pool their capital and spread their risk. Some amounted to insurance policies. Others were realized through carefully designed contracts between one partner without capital who did the venturing abroad, and the other who provided the capital but stayed at home. In many cases, several investors would lend funds to a "venture merchant" at a high interest rate, but with the principal and interest payable only upon the cargo's safe delivery. Thus the venture merchant assumed the normal risks associated with any commercial endeavor, while the investors accepted the risks associated with shipwreck or piracy in return for a set fee. These tools were employed in increasingly complicated ways as merchants developed ever more ingenious means of managing capital risk.[21]

Institutionalizing Capital

New financial tools, however, were never going to be enough. Also necessary were institutions that used these devices in imaginative ways. This was provided by forms of banking—deposit, exchange, and investment banking—that didn't differ in their essentials from modern banking practices.

One of the Commercial Revolution's most important features was a remarkable growth in the available amounts of capital in the form of equity and debt, the trading of money and credit, and the demand for commercial loans. Certainly the amount of capital available in this period should not be exaggerated. The overall money supply between 1300 and 1500 appears to have been low.[22] The output of mints, the availability of bullion, and money in circulation, however, dramatically increased throughout Europe.[23] The church's extensive land assets, for instance, were dwarfed by the liquid assets at its disposal.[24]

The practice of accepting money and other commodities as a simple deposit had been maintained throughout Europe after the fall of Rome, usually by monasteries. During the early Middle Ages, some of the most prominent depositaries were military religious orders, such as the Knights Hospitallers (today's Order of Malta), who, because of their truly international character, regularly transferred large amounts of money and lent out considerable sums to credit-worthy borrowers.[25] Many monasteries also made loans,[26] often to each other but also to rulers who pledged land as a security. On many occasions, interest was charged.[27] The same monasteries and even dioceses became involved in the sale of annuities. These were considered to fall outside the bounds of the usury laws because it was acknowledged they involved a degree of risk.[28]

Over time, the simple deposit came to be accompanied by other forms of deposits. One was the "time deposit." This involved depositing a sum of money for a certain period of time. This was then returned not with interest but rather with a discretionary gift from the banker to the client[29]—though sometimes, as Raymond de Roover states, "interest at a given rate per year was openly stipulated."[30] Another was the deposit as investment. Initially this practice was localized, but soon assumed more sophisticated form as northern Italian Catholic merchant-bankers, such as the Medici and Bardi families, expanded their operations.

Some of these institutions began as moneychangers—an essential activity in a Europe in which there were numerous coinages in circulation and ongoing concerns about possible tampering with their weight and metallic composition.[31] Ongoing difficulties included securing the safety of money and the desire of those who placed their money in banks to add to or reduce their monetary holdings at irregular intervals. This led to the development of negotiable paper as a way of avoiding transferring bullion between cities.[32] Such paper facilitated the development of banking devices such as the check, the drawing account, and the bill of exchange. The bill of exchange proved to be especially significant because it could be purchased at a date before it fell due at a discount somewhat less than its face value—the difference usually being the buyer's fee.

From here, it was not a stretch for these same banks to become involved in international money transfers. This included the wealth received and dispensed by a papacy that was assuming a greater religious and political role throughout Europe. Banks sold letters of credit and bills of exchange to traveling merchants, pilgrims, and clergy that could be redeemed by a named beneficiary or the issuer. They were also used as conduits for life annuities, mutual funds, and share ownership of limited-liability corporations. These Christian-owned and -operated financial operations dwarfed those of most Jewish moneylenders, the majority of the latter being focused on pawnbroking and minor consumption loans.[33]

Much of this business was transacted through personal relationships with credit operations being mediated through private contracts between lenders and borrowers.[34] To expedite the efficiency of these transactions, Italian banking families established clearing-house operations and transfer banks in Europe's important commercial centers.[35] They subsequently opened branches throughout Europe in cities such as Barcelona, Avignon, Bruges, Geneva, Lyons, London, Hamburg, and Antwerp.[36] Thus, as Rodney Stark writes,

> By the thirteenth century there were 38 independent banks in Florence, 34 in Pisa, 27 in Genoa, 18 in Venice—a combined total of 173 in the leading Italian city-states. Most of these Italian banks had foreign branches. In 1231 there were 69 Italian banking branches operating in England and nearly as many in Ireland. In fact, until well into the fifteenth century every bank in Western Europe was either in Italy or was a branch of an Italian bank.[37]

These private banks in what has been called a growing "international republic of money"[38]— Italian and Greek transfer banks operated as far east as Constantinople until 1453[39]—didn't just pay interest on deposits. They also used such deposits as a basis for furnishing interest-bearing loans to those parts of Europe that lacked capital. Some loans were given out by banks for long-term purposes to businesses and governments. Like modern businessmen, many merchants took out short-term loans to cover cash-flow gaps or fund particular short-term projects.[40]

At any one time, banks that dealt with time deposits and uncondi-
tional deposits were likely to maintain less than 100 percent reserves
because bankers needed to invest the long-term deposits in order
to recover the interest they paid to depositors and return a profit.[41]
Many medieval banks thus effectively created deposits, insofar as
they lent out more than they held. The fact, however, that this "ghost
money" existed only on balance sheets meant that money was no longer simply a physical reality in the form of coinage made from precious metals.

The emergence of "ghost money" raised questions of what might
happen when depositors' demands exceeded a bank's holdings of
money on hand. Many governments passed laws to protect depositors.[42] There was, we should recall, no lender of last resort in this
world, and the rate of bank failure was subsequently high.

It isn't an exaggeration to say that all these changes amounted to
the emergence of the world's first relatively sophisticated money and
capital markets. Such was the pace of growth that it escaped the dominance of Italians relatively quickly. By the early seventeenth century,
they were complaining to the Grand Duke of Florence that they were
no longer "the masters of the money of other countries."[43] This inter-
nationalization of finance both followed and forwarded the proto-
globalization of European economies.

The Not-So-Dark Ages

Even the brief sketch of medieval economic life outlined above con-
tradicts the standard "Dark Ages" mythologies that prevail in contemporary writing about the Middle Ages. Schumpeter did not exag-
gerate when he wrote that "by the end of the fifteenth century most
of the phenomena that we are in the habit of associating with that
vague word 'Capitalism' had put in their appearance, including big
business, stock and commodity speculation, and 'high finance.'"[44]
Life in medieval Europe remained shorter and less comfortable compared to twenty-first-century developed economies. No one, however, who has spent any time in Florence and other northern Italian
medieval towns such as Venice and Genoa or the market squares of

Bruges, Antwerp, and Brussels can deny either the genuine civilizational advances that occurred during this period or the economic and financial changes that made them possible.

But also present was a specific consciousness, including among many of Christianity's best minds, that capital was crucial to the very possibility of doing business in this new economic environment. St. Antoninus of Florence (1389–1459) stated, for instance, that while money as a form of circulating coin or medium of exchange might be sterile, money-as-capital was *not* sterile, not least because it was a necessary precondition for embarking on business.[45]

Nor can we forget that Western Europe remained an intensely religious society in the midst of all this commercial activity. The church continued to be the most significant institutional and cultural force that transcended Europe's internal political divisions. As the medievalist Henri Pirenne once observed, the church "was not only the great moral authority of the age, but also the great financial power."[46] For many years, it was the only place where you could find men capable of tracking revenue and expenditure, keeping accounts, and balancing them.[47]

Many of the markets and towns that emerged in the wake of the Commercial Revolution initially developed around such monasteries. The inhabitants of cities would often declare themselves the "serfs" of the town's patron saint.[48] In other cases, clergy—including many Franciscans—gravitated to cities because this was where they found increasing numbers of their flocks. More and more people, freed from the struggle just to survive, had the time and resources to engage the world of ideas. It was thus no coincidence that the medieval period witnessed the church creating and building the world's first universities in cities, ranging from Bologna to Oxford, Salerno, Paris, Prague, and St. Andrews.

From the beginning these institutions were based on a belief that God existed, that he had made man in his image, and that people had to be free to seek the truth through logic, attention to evidence, careful scholarship, and free discussion. As it turns out, part of that search for truth—the truth about the nature of things, but also the truth about doing good and evil—involved the exploration of the new economic things of the time, including the emerging markets for capital, by scholastic theologians.

Noonan goes so far as to describe the scholastic investigation of usury and moneylending as amounting to the development of "an embryonic theory of economics."[49] What is especially noteworthy about the work of scholastic theologians is that they didn't simply speculate about these matters. "They did," Schumpeter remarks, "all the fact-finding that it was possible for them to do in an age without statistical services. Their generalizations invariably grew out of the discussion of factual patterns and were copiously illustrated by practical examples."[50]

Back to Aristotle—and Rome

Many of the financial tools and institutions that emerged during the Commercial Revolution depended on a willingness to charge and pay interest. There were, however, objections to this by many theologians.

The first was the ancient objection spelled out in Scripture: the wrongness of moneylenders exploiting the poor. In the words of the thirteenth-century French scholastic thinker William of Auxerre, usury was "contrary to that species of justice which obliges us to relieve a neighbor in need."[51] Despite the decline of relative poverty in the wake of the economic growth that followed the rise of commerce, legitimate concerns remained that moneylending might put at risk the principle that the poor should have access to money in times of need.

Attention to the same economic growth, however, helped broaden Christian moral analysis beyond the poverty issue. Greater focus was given to the *intentionality* with which someone loaned money as well as the intrinsic nature of lending and borrowing. The new conditions of relatively competitive markets for money and capital also raised urgent questions about the price of capital: in other words, the justice or otherwise of a *market* rate of interest.[52]

A second set of problems confronted by the scholastics arose from the revival of Aristotelian thought in Western Europe. Aristotle's ideas had never completely disappeared. Indeed, knowledge of the full corpus of Aristotle's thought became more widespread as more manuscripts were brought to the West from the Orthodox world by merchants, soldiers, scholars, and clergy, and the ideas they contained circulated more freely in royal courts, universities, and monasteries.[53] Renewed attention to Aristotle, however, meant that theologians were obliged to reconsider Aristotle's claim that moneylending in itself was a perversion of the use of money.

It was not that scholastic thinkers didn't think money could not increase. Looking around, they saw that it obviously could. Rather it was, as the Norman Franciscan and one-time Lord Chancellor of England Richard of Middleton (1249–1302) wrote, a matter of money being perverted from its proper purpose of being a price, medium, and measure in buying and selling other things.[54] Closely connected to this was the claim that moneylenders were making profits without expending any labor of their own.

Yet the return to Aristotle also provided another means for thinking about money that helped clarify the justice or otherwise of a given loan. Given that moneylending was a commercial transaction, it fell squarely under the criterion of one of the aspects of justice identified by Aristotle: commutative justice—the justice that governs contracts freely entered into by two or more persons.[55] Commutative justice also involves, for instance, considering who in a given transaction is *entitled* to what—whether by the nature of the case or because of some extrinsic title.

It was thus possible for interest payments to become understood as a way of reestablishing the balance of justice between lenders and borrowers by *restoring* a lender's financial position to make up the difference (the Latin *inter-est* means "in between" and "difference") between what was likely to be returned and what was given. Thus, as prominent a medieval figure as the Dominican canonist St. Raymond of Penafort (1175–1275) was able to define interest as "not profit, but the avoidance of loss."[56]

A further complication emerged as a consequence of merchants, canonists, and civil lawyers turning to Roman law to find ways of legally ordering the commercial bustle around them. According to

Roman law, one could not charge interest on the loan of a fungible good—the *mutuum*[57] (from *meum tuum*: mine becomes thine)— because it implied a transfer of ownership of a *res fungibilis*: that is, something measurable in quantity and quality that was consumed in use and thus couldn't be used creatively. Hence, if borrowed, a *mutuum* could only be restored in the *exact* kind and quantity. The debtor's only responsibility was to repay the precise amount received: one orange for one orange. It was consequently not permissible to charge interest on a loan of money as a fungible good.[58]

Seneca's objection that usurers were in the business of selling time also resurfaced in the medieval period. Time, the argument went, belonged to God. Hence, as the thirteenth-century English theologian Thomas of Chobham wrote, "The usurer does not sell the debtor something which is his own, but time, which belongs to God. It follows that because he sells something belonging to another he ought not to have any profit from it."[59] Despite these objections and the regular denouncements of moneylenders (often laced with ferociously anti-Semitic remarks) by many Christian clergy, it's revealing that the church prosecuted very few cases of usury. This may owe something to the fact that many clergy were themselves involved in moneylending.[60] Reluctance to prosecute, however, may have also proceeded from another factor.

Certainly everyone believed that usury *qua* usury was sinful. In 1179, the Third Lateran Council condemned what it called "notorious usurers," ordering them to make restitution.[61] The question, however, that Christians found themselves asking was: "What *is* usury?" St. Bernardine argued, for instance, that "all usury is profit, but not all profit is usury."[62]

Reflecting on the definition of usury was an invitation to make intellectual distinctions that addressed some of the issues noted above, but in ways that maintained Christianity's condemnation of usury. Bernardine's underscoring of the difference between money-as-money and money-as-capital is a good illustration. This opened up the possibility of distinguishing between (1) consumption loans and (2) loans of capital in the context of economic growth rather than subsistence economies.

God's Time, My Time

It did not take long for medieval theologians and canonists to start examining the various questions about moneylending that took on a whole new dimension in the context of the Commercial Revolution. One such issue was whether moneylending involved selling what is not ours to sell: that is, time.

Some medieval thinkers began by asking whether all time did in fact belong to God. In one sense, they concluded, this is certainly true. To this day, the Easter liturgy of the Orthodox and Catholic churches identifies Christ as the Alpha and the Omega, the beginning and the end, to whom all time belongs.

The same scholars, however, argued that every person has to make free choices about how he uses the specific time allocated to him. This was the position taken by the fourteenth-century minister-general of the Franciscan Order, Gerald Odonis. "In the first sense," he wrote, "time is something common and in no way vendible. In the second sense it is the property of someone, just as a year of a horse lent me is said to be mine."[63] From this perspective, charging someone for the time-use of something becomes more plausible.

It had been recognized for centuries that money was not simply a measure but also a store of value: something that could be accumulated and deployed elsewhere in the future. Aristotle had long ago illustrated how money overcame the problem of exchange through time: if we don't want something right now, money enables us to have it if we ever do need it.[64]

But what if the price for something in the future was likely to be greater than in the present? Considering this very question, Pope Gregory IX's decretal *Naviganti*, of 1234 (compiled by Raymond of Penafort), stated it was permissible to charge a higher price where payment was being deferred over time *if* significant questions existed concerning the good's future price.[65]

The implications of this statement for charging interest were considerable. It suggested that a seller of money might be entitled to indemnify himself against the risk that a price rise might occur between the time of the loan and the time of the loan's repayment.

It also indicated that if the lender is entitled to receive back the full value of what was given at the time of the loan, more units of money might have to be paid back in the future. Interest was one way of making up the difference in a stable way, thus restoring equity. This point was grasped by one of Thomas Aquinas's students, Giles of Lessines (1230–1304). In his *De usuris*, he maintained that some could in fact ask for a higher price for a credit sale, provided no dishonesty or fraud was involved.[66]

Work, Creativity, and Money

Another part of the puzzle that began to be resolved in the medieval period was how human work could render money fertile. Every Jew and Christian knew from Scripture's very first pages that humans were not made to be passive. Everyone was called on to help realize the potential of what God had given human beings to cultivate. The way to do this was through work.

Perhaps it was due to new conditions of economic growth, but medieval Christians began to apply this classic Jewish and Christian emphasis to finance. Could it be that, through work, money could be rendered fertile? The first medieval to state this explicitly was Richard of Middleton. In exploring the issue of legitimate profit, he looked carefully at the issue of money's sterility:

> Of a sterile thing no one ought to demand a fruit, but money of itself is a sterile thing, for it can bring forth no fruit *except* by the labor and solicitude of the user; therefore you ought not to demand any fruit of your money *if* you have neither labored nor been solicitous for that profit.[67]

In his forty-second Lenten sermon, *Interest, or in What Cases It Is Licit to Receive beyond the Principal*, St. Bernardine argued that the merchant who lends money may ask for compensation for foregone profits because he "gives not money in its simple character, but he also gives his capital."[68] Operative, however, in Bernardine's analysis was an implicit attention to how work made money fruitful:

[I]t is to be said that money was truly worth more to its owner than itself because of the industry with which he would have used it. . . . [T]hat money has value not from itself, but from the owner's industry. And therefore the receiver of the money not only deprives the owner of his money, but also of all the use and fruit of exercising his industry in it and through it.[69]

In a similar fashion, Gerald Odonis considered whether the labor of borrower or the labor of lender should receive compensation. He concluded that the lender's labor certainly was at stake. Taking the voice of the lender, Gerald specified: "I say that I do not sell you your industry but sell you the cessation of my own industry, which to me is harmful and to you profitable. For we cannot both use the same money at the same time."[70]

Partnership and Investment in a Growth Economy

It was, however, the greatest medieval theologian, Thomas Aquinas, who made some of the most decisive contributions to developing Christian teaching on finance. Though influenced by Aristotle, Aquinas rejected "the Philosopher's" view that those involved in commerce would become obsessed with their own riches and unconcerned with the common good.[71] Instead Aquinas held that it was entirely possible for people to engage in commerce, and with correct intentions such as the desire to help the needy or take care of one's family.[72]

Aquinas invested considerable effort in examining how one determined the justice of a given commercial transaction, how one measured the value of a good, and what constituted a just price. In his view, it was normally the case that the measure of something's value is the price it would presently fetch "in the market" [*secundum commune forum*].[73] This was understood as the exchanges between willing buyers and sellers in the same place and time frame, with all parties to the exchange being aware of the merits and defects of what is being exchanged.[74] Significantly, Aquinas specified that this market price will vary from time to time and location to location, depending on whether the good is scarce or abundant [*secundum diversitatem copiae et inopiae rerum*].[75] He also insisted that sellers who enter the marketplace do not violate justice if they sell a commodity at the available price knowing that the price will fall when other sellers come to market, provided that they deceive no one.[76] Though Aquinas never disputed that the state can act to regulate prices in emergencies,[77] he held that the just price is normally the market price in the absence of fraud or collusion.

Inevitably Aquinas came face to face with the question of what, if anything, I can legitimately charge for the use of my money. Certainly Aquinas objected to charging interest on loans of *mutuum*. But he also identified two titles external to the loan itself that justified a return to the lender that exceeded the principal. Finnis summarizes Aquinas's titles in the following way:

> (1) *Share of profits in joint enterprises.* If I "lend" my money to a merchant or craftsman on the basis that we are in partnership [*societas*] . . . so that I am to share in any overall losses or profits, my entitlement to my dividend of the profits (as well as to the return of my capital *if its value has not been lost by the joint enterprise*) is just and appropriate. (2) *Recompense or indemnity* [*interesse*] *for losses.* In making any loan I can levy a charge on the borrower in order to compensate me for whatever expenses I have outlaid or losses I have incurred by making the loan. And the terms of a loan can include a fee or charge which is payable if you fail to repay the principal on time, and is sufficient to compensate me for the losses I am liable to incur if the principal is not repaid on time.[78]

The most striking feature of Aquinas's two titles for justly recovering something beyond the principal is its compatibility with the development of a market in loans of money at a market rate of interest. How so? Finnis explains this in the following way:

> With the development of a genuine investment market, in which stocks and shares (i.e., association in the risks of pro-

ductive and other commercial enterprise) are traded alongside
bonds (transferable money loans), it becomes possible to identify a rate of interest on bonds and other loans which compen-
sates lenders for what they are reasonably presumed to have
lost by making the loan rather than investing their money, for
profit, in shares. Indeed, an efficient market will tend to identify this indemnifying rate of interest automatically.[79]

Many scholastic theologians quickly saw that a foregone gain
could be an actual loss when you're living in an economy in which
opportunities for gain are part of everyday life. Schumpeter points
out that this meant two things:

> First, merchants themselves who hold money for business pur-
> poses, evaluating this money with reference to expected gain,
> were considered justified in charging interest both on outright
> loans and in cases of deferred payment for commodities. Sec-
> ond, if the opportunity for gain contingent on the possession
> of money is quite general or, in other words, if there is a money
> market, then everyone, even if not in business himself, may
> accept the interest determined by the market mechanism.[80]

Just Titles to Interest

The Commercial Revolution was thus accompanied by a growing
Christian recognition that while a *mutuum* excluded the possibility
of charging interest on the basis of an *intrinsic* title to the loan itself,
it was possible to justify interest on grounds not adherent to the contract itself. Christian theologians subsequently identified four such
extrinsic titles:

1. First, there was the payment of a penalty if money was not
   repaid in time. This was known as a *poena conventionalis*: the
   difference between what had been due and what was paid. Such
   a fine was the "interest." Once this was accepted, it became

accepted practice to place penalty clauses against such delays into contracts.

2. It was possible that a lender could suffer real damages because of the borrower's failure to return the capital on the schedule determined by the contract. Hence the lender could claim what was called a *damnum emergens* (actual monetary loss incurred). Significantly this title was accepted as legitimate by figures preceding Aquinas, such as his master St. Albertus Magnus.[81]

3. A lender could claim for the loss of a possible profit (*lucrum cessans*) if he missed the opportunity of making a profit as a result of lending it to others. Over time, this would become virtually synonymous with *interesse*.[82]

4. There was a legitimate payment that the lender could charge for the risk of losing his capital (*periculum sortis*).[83] Some medieval thinkers emphasized just how damaging a borrower's failure to repay the lender's loan could be to the latter. In his *Summa Confessorum*, for instance, Thomas de Chobham presented a sympathetic portrait of a creditor who lost everything because someone to whom he lent money had defaulted.[84]

Note that in all these cases, it remained wrong to charge interest on a loan by virtue of the very making of the loan. This, however, was perfectly compatible with maintaining that moneylenders could fairly charge for other factors. These included risk of nonpayment, probable inflation, taxes, the costs incurred in making and administering the loan, and the forgoing of other legitimate uses to which the money could have been put. Hence, it was with little difficulty that the last ecumenical council in the West before the Reformation, the Fifth Lateran Council (1512–1517), could define usury as "nothing else than gain or profit drawn from the use of a thing that is by its nature sterile, a profit acquired *without labor, costs, or risk*."[85] Not only did these words imply that money wasn't always sterile or a consumable fungible; they also underscored the insight that risk, labor, and costs provided a basis for receiving back more than the principal.

Spreading the Risk

So what remained of the condemnation of usury? The prohibition of levying exorbitant interest rates on the poor stressed in Scripture and the Church Fathers was still in place. Scholastic thinkers also continued arguing among themselves about the scope of the titles. Could interest be justified only on the grounds of extrinsic titles? Or was it in fact possible to charge on an intrinsic title? For practical purposes, however, it amounted to the same thing. In terms of the development of finance, what matters is that these intellectual explorations, as Diana Wood notes, "sanctioned many of the monetary considerations that underlie modern economies."[86]

One effect of all these intellectual developments was to help shift the epicenter of economic life away from a focus on natural resources and agriculture to one in which capital and finance played a central role. The new attitudes about money also steered liquid capital away from consumption loans and toward economically productive enterprises. Noonan, for instance, contends that "it is probable that the scholastic theory may have encouraged bankers to participate as risk-sharers in commercial ventures."[87]

The debate about usury also yielded a number of devices that helped spur the ever-growing sophistication of the economy's financial sector. Especially significant in this connection was the manner in which the usury discussion before and after the Reformation facilitated the use of a financial device known as the "triple contract."

Beginning with the development of property insurance for maritime merchants, the basic outline of the *contractus trinus* was first proposed by the vicar-general of the Franciscans of the Observance in 1485, Angelus Carletus de Clavasio (1411–1495). He insisted it was licit for one member of a business partnership to insure his capital with a third party.[88]

In very simple terms, the triple contract amounted to a combined package of insurance, a partnership, and a sales contract. The first was an investment contract and partnership for a specified period of time in a particular venture in which it was assumed that the investment would yield a specified profit. A London merchant would thus invest 2,000 pounds for one year in a given enterprise on the assumption that it would produce a 10 percent profit of 200 pounds in that period, but no more than that.

The second contract was an insurance contract on the amount of the principal of the investment. The investor would pay the premium from the profits of the investment contract. The premium of the policy on the example cited above would thus be 5 percent of the investment, or 100 pounds. The third contract was for a specified return on the investment that was paid to the investor out of the profits from the investment contract. In other words, the future uncertain (high) gain was traded for a more certain (lower) gain.

As a financial device, triple contracts allowed their participants to hedge their risk in the face of uncertainty over time and still realize a profit. It amounted to selling an uncertain future gain for a certain lesser gain (that being a guarantee of a fixed return based on a percentage rate). It also allowed contracted partners to create a contract of insurance for the principal investment in return for an assignment of the future probable gain from the partnership.[89]

The increasing use of triple contracts introduced greater stability into business partnerships. Nor did it take long for canny investors looking to further diversify risk to realize that one way of doing so was to make the three contracts with different persons. In practical terms, the transactions involved in the triple contract were only distinguished from those of a loan by the designation for a business purpose of the funds conveyed by the triple contract. Those justifying the contract invoked the extrinsic title of *lucrum cessans*, arguing that it was always present in such arrangements.

The triple contract's morality did not go undisputed. Some theologians argued that it constituted covert usury. Others, however, defended it, the most notable being Father Johannes Eck (1486–1543). A lecturer in theology in Augsburg, Eck lived in a city full of financial houses, not least among which was the Fugger family, who were, by this point, the papacy's bankers.[90] Examining criticisms of the triple contract, Eck held that it was not usury. Divine summarizes Eck's underlying logic as follows: "Since it is lawful to make a profit from an enterprise involving risk and (2) the larger the risk the larger would be the profit allowed, therefore (3) it should be lawful for a man to contract for a low rate of interest on his capital in return for the security of the capital involved."[91]

Eck was astute enough to direct his most complete defenses of this position not only to merchants and clergy but also to one of Europe's most important centers of learning, the University of Bologna, where he presented his views before an audience of some of Europe's leading theologians and canonists. Here Eck insisted that the industry associated with money was productive. Hence, the investor who "gives the commodity of his capital" (the language is revealing) was owed his share.[92]

Eck was, however, unable to continue in this endeavor. By 1520, he found himself embroiled in the great theological debates occasioned by Martin Luther. He subsequently emerged as one of Luther's most formidable opponents.

Eck's defense of the triple contract was nevertheless important for four reasons. First, the very fact that Eck defended the contract underscored just how open one of the most orthodox of theologians was to financial innovations. Second, Eck's expositions amounted to the most public explanation of the triple contract's workings not just to theologians but also to men of commerce. Third, Eck's prestige as one of Catholic orthodoxy's most prominent defenders in the wake of the Reformation helped his arguments gain wide acceptance throughout the Catholic world. So too did the fourth effect: that in analyzing Eck's analysis of the triple contract, the enormously influential Dominican cardinal, Tomas de Cajetan (1469–1534) concluded that the triple contract was preferable to outright usury.[93]

Money Markets, and Speculation

Like all debates concerning usury, discussion of the triple contract continued for years afterward. The most dynamic of post-Reformation religious orders, the Jesuits, took a particular interest in the subject. In his *De iustitia et iure*, for example, the Flemish Jesuit Leonard Lessius (1554–1623) engaged in a cost–benefit analysis of the triple contract and outlined the economic case for investment of private wealth in safe commercial credit contracts for the sake of making profit.

By helping bankers and investors manage risk, the triple contract played a significant role in the growth of important money markets in cities such as Lyons, Antwerp, and Amsterdam. These facilitated an increased availability of credit for businesses working across national boundaries as well as large loans for governments strapped for cash.

The growth of money markets led to individuals and banks speculating on money itself. Indeed, the very fact that exchange rates fluctuated meant that it was impossible for a moneychanger to make a riskless profit.[94] Part of the Christian intellectual contribution to these developments was the realization that money itself was not a fixed measure of the value of other goods. In his *Comentario resolutoio de usuras* (1556), written as an appendix to a penitential manual on moral theology, Martin de Azpilcueta articulated what amounted to one of the first quantity theories of money. The scholastics understood very well that the quantity of money circulating in an economy affected prices.[95] This was especially obvious in the wake of influx of precious metals from America into Europe from the early sixteenth century onward. Some commentators estimate that these importations tripled prices between 1500 and 1600.[96]

According to Azpilcueta, the value of money was not fixed because it varied according to the supply (i.e., quantity) available. "All merchandise," he stated, "becomes dearer when it is in great demand and short supply, and that money, in so far as it may be sold, bartered, or exchanged by some other form of contract, is merchandise, and therefore also becomes dearer when it is in great demand and short supply."[97] Hence Azpilcueta wrote, "Money is worth more where and when it is scarce than where and when it is abundant. . . . And it may be concluded that money is more valuable in one country than another, and more valuable at one time than at another."[98]

This meant that there was no objection, in principle, to speculation on money. As Molina pointed out, significant legitimate profit could be realized if an exchange dealer was clever enough to "conjecture the place and time, in which money will be worth much more, because of the lack of it and the necessity for it of the merchants and others."[99]

What separated speculators from usurers, in Molina's view, was that speculators could not be certain of a profit. If usury involved risk-free, certain gain on a loan, then the *uncertain* character of speculation with regard to exchange dealings rendered speculation legitimate in the eyes of scholastic thinkers.[100] The justification for speculative profit thus lay in the *risk* undertaken by the speculator. Moreover, such speculation was a form of *work*. Though it was not manual labor, speculation was no different from that of the mental work undertaken by, for instance, investors. Molina also saw this form of speculation as serving the real economy inasmuch as it helped direct money and capital to those places and persons in the economy where it is needed but not yet present.

These ideas did not amount to a Christian justification of every single activity associated with speculation. In his seventeenth-century treatise on business *Il negotiante*, the Italian merchant and proto-economist Giovanni Domenico Peri singled out as reprehensible those bankers who tried to manipulate exchange rates in order to create artificial rigidities in the money market. Peri also described the practice of spreading rumors in order to speculate on prices as a species of fraud.[101] In this connection, he invoked and echoed high church authorities. Sixty years earlier, Pope Pius V had formally condemned such practices.[102] The sins listed here, however, are not derived from speculation itself. Rather, they involve other moral errors such as deceit and lying.

Toward the Full Justification of Interest

The Reformation made little difference to the discussion of finance among Christians. Prominent Anglican and Puritan divines, for instance, such as William Ames (1576–1633) and Thomas Wilson (1525–1581) did not significantly differ from Catholic thinkers on issues of money, interest, exchange, price, and interest.[103] Jordan Ballor has illustrated that while a division of opinion within the Protestant and Catholic worlds reigned between those who had less restrictive and more constricted views of these issues, the division didn't break down along confessional lines.[104] The real argument, as Divine summarizes, was

> whether in the face of changed economic conditions it was still necessary to have recourse to the old roundabout method of extrinsic titles to justify the taking of interest, or whether the practice could be considered justifiable on the basis of the intrinsic nature of the loan. This latter position came to be defended by both Protestant and Catholic writers who based their conclusions on the fertility or quasi-fertility or quasi-productivity of money under modern economic conditions.[105]

At least one Protestant theologian expressed forceful but also somewhat contradictory views about usury. On the one hand, Luther engaged in sweeping denunciations of moneylending per se and attacked the theory of extrinsic titles as a mere sophism.[106] On other occasions, however, Luther made exceptions consistent with preceding tradition, most notably when loans were used for a profitable enterprise.[107] Luther's collaborator Philipp Melanchthon (1497–1560) didn't hesitate to invoke the scholastic distinction between fungible and nonfungible goods when discussing the issue. He also affirmed that interest could be charged for *lucrum cessans* and *damnum emergens*.[108]

An exception to this pattern was John Calvin (1509–1564). Like the scholastics, he began with the principle of equity in exchange. But Calvin dismissed outright the Aristotelian notion concerning money's sterility. Calvin was also critical of the various interest titles established by Catholics and affirmed by Protestants. Such titles were, Calvin said, mere disguises for usury and might well be used as a basis for charging interest on the poor. That said, the differences between Calvin and the scholastics should not be exaggerated. What Calvin permits by way of charging interest in business transactions, for instance, is not different in substance from what Eck allowed with the triple contract.[109]

Calvin was, however, no laxist with regard to moneylending. He was unenthusiastic about the practice in general—so much so that he thought "habitual moneylenders" should be expelled from church and society. Calvin's approach to finance was to focus on the Golden Rule's demands: that is, do unto others as they would do unto you. Any money contract that violated this principle, he stated, was invalid. On this basis, Calvin argued that (1) profit on any loan to the poor is evil; (2) any profit on the loan to the rich person or businessman must be no more than that of a seller's on a sale; (3) profit on a loan that involves no risk on the lender's part is usury; (4) the lender should not enjoy a greater profit than the borrower; and (5) charging interest to rich merchants who borrow to increase their profits is lawful.

Calvin's disciple Molinaeus was less dismissive of the scholastic analysis. The creditor, he argued, experienced some loss or foregone compensation in virtually every loan. This entitled creditors to *interesse*. Molinaeus also stressed that money, like land, could only become productive through work. These and similar ideas were taken up by Calvinist and Catholic banking families in the Netherlands and codified into Dutch civil law in 1658.[110]

By the mid-eighteenth century, a consensus had arisen throughout Europe about these matters. Summarizing the position during this period, the historian Werner Sombart states,

> The very simple formula in which ecclesiastical authority expressed its attitude to the question of profit making is this: Interest on a pure money loan, in any form, is forbidden; profit on capital, in any form, is permitted, whether it flows from commercial business, or from an industrial undertaking . . . or from insurance against transport risks; or from shareholding in an enterprise . . . or however else.[111]

The expression of this teaching throughout Protestant and Catholic Europe continued, however, to be articulated in negative terms. With the Industrial Revolution's advent and the subsequent expansion and use of capital, there was an increase of questions about usury and requests for clarifications from church authorities. Between 1822 and 1836, the congregation of the Roman Curia responsible for overseeing Catholic teaching on faith and morals, the Holy Office (today's Congregation for the Doctrine of the Faith), issued a series of decrees. These settled the matter for any Catholic lender worried whether he had a just title by simply stating that the interest allowed by law was permissible. The working assumption was that the loan was just, and usury the exception rather than the rule.[112]

Though no sources are cited in the decrees, there seems little doubt they were influenced by a posthumous book, *Dissertation sur le prêt-de-commerce* (1822), written by a French prelate, Cardinal Guillaume de la Luzerne (1738–1821). His argument stated that, as far as Christian dogma was concerned, usury amounted to oppressive or excessive profit on a loan. The cardinal also specified that usury's sinfulness involved the wrongfulness of exploiting the poor through loans. Most importantly, Luzerne underscored that business loans were completely different from *mutuum* loans for consumption: the value of the business loan, he wrote, will in fact "increase by the use one makes of it." Luzerne made a point of saying that his arguments were largely the same made by Eck in defense of the triple contract almost three hundred years earlier.[113]

Tradition and Innovation

How then are we to summarize the history of Christian teaching on usury, loans, and interest? With reference to the church, which has maintained the most sustained analysis of the subject, Noonan states the following at the end of his long book on this topic:

> As far as dogma in the technical Catholic sense is concerned, there is only one dogma at stake: that usury, *the act of taking profit on a loan without just title, is sinful.* . . . This dogmatic teaching remains unchanged. What is just title, what is technically to be treated as a loan, are matters of debate, positive law, and changing evaluation. The development on these points is great. But the pure and narrow dogma is the same today as in 1200.[114]

The process by which Christians developed the world's understanding of some of contemporary finance's most basic building blocks yielded considerable fruit of a conceptual, practical, and institutional nature. The interplay between economic conditions and ideas in the Christian world wasn't, however, limited to reflection on private finance. It also produced lasting contributions to thinking about the state's responsibilities in this area.

Further Reading

Azevedo Alves, André, and José Manuel Moreira. *The Salamanca School*. London: Continuum, 2010.

Chafuen, Alejandro A. *Faith and Liberty: The Economic Thought of the Late-Scholastics*. Lanham, MD: Lexington Books, 2003.

Dempsey, Bernard W., S.J. *Interest and Usury*. London: Dennis Dobson, 1948.

Noonan, John T. *The Scholastic Analysis of Usury*. Cambridge, MA: Harvard University Press, 1957.

Wood, Diana. *Medieval Economic Thought*. Cambridge: Cambridge University Press, 2002.

4

Caesar's Coin

"Why do you set this trap for me? Hand me a denarius and let me see it." They handed him one and he said to them, "Whose head is this? Whose name?" "Caesar's," they told him. Jesus said to them, "Give back to Caesar what belongs to Caesar—and to God what belongs to God." This reply took them completely by surprise.

Mark 12:15–17

The New Testament accounts of the attempt to trap Christ into either affirming Roman authority to levy taxes on his fellow Jews or placing himself in opposition to that very same authority have been correctly understood as representing the beginning of Christianity's de-deification of the state. Paul's and Peter's letters make clear that the early church taught Christians to respect state authority. Christianity, however, was equally firm that neither Caesar nor the state were gods.

There is a strong likelihood that the coin shown to Christ was a Roman denarius stamped with the image of Emperor Tiberius and the words *Ti[berius] Caesar Divi Aug[usti] F[ilius] Augustus* ["Caesar Augustus Tiberius, son of the Divine Augustus"]. The Roman state's use of this currency was not simply a question of providing its subjects with an economic tool that would be accepted by all. The impressing of the emperor's image on the coin was also a claim to supreme authority, even a type of divine sovereignty—so much so that the Jews refused to allow Roman coins to circulate in the Temple (hence, the need for moneychangers at the Temple's entrance).

One reason given for the state's monopoly of the money supply is that such control is an expression of sovereignty. The scholar
who most developed the modern concept of sovereignty, Jean Bodin
(1530–1596), identified the right to issue coinage as a key element of
sovereignty, not least because he thought the state should reserve to
itself the authority to alter the value of money.[1]

This question of sovereignty looms large in contemporary debates
about government's specific responsibilities vis-à-vis the financial
sector. In the early twenty-first century, some of the most conten-
tious discussions surrounding the Euro concerned its impact upon
European Union (EU) member-states' national sovereignty. Likewise, much of the reaction against the Pontifical Council for Justice
and Peace's 2011 Note on global financial structures arose from the
Council's linkage between the possibility of creating a global central
bank and the apparent diminishment of the nation-state's authority.

In practice, government monopolies of currencies have seldom
been total. When Adam Smith listed what he regarded as the
state's three primary economic responsibilities, he didn't include
the money supply. The sociologist Geoffrey Ingham points out that
"coinages circulated promiscuously across ill-defined and insecure
jurisdictions in later medieval Europe; local money was issued as late
as the mid-nineteenth century in Europe; and capitalist networks
have always developed their own 'private' media and means of payment—'near money' such as certificates of deposit."[2] A multiplicity
of media of exchange, ranging from private bank money to corporate and government script, operated side by side in early industrialized economies.[3]

Today state institutions are involved in the financial sector in ways
that go far beyond currency issues. In all countries, various authorities regulate different parts of the financial industry. Central banks
set official interest rates and intervene in other ways in economic life
to the extent that some describe them as constituting a fourth branch
of government.[4]

What, however, is a Christian to think about the state's role
with regard to money and finance more generally? At first glance, it

might seem that, beyond broad exhortations to punish fraud and not neglect the poor's well-being when determining monetary policy and designing financial regulations, Christians have relatively little to say.

Historically speaking, it's true that, compared to the questions addressed in the previous chapter, Christians have given less attention to these subjects. Over the centuries, however, some theologians have addressed the state's role in shaping the economy's financial sector. Scholastic thinkers even argued among themselves as to whether governments should require banks to maintain a 100-percent reserve.[5] Much of this commentary parallels the rise of the modern state and associated concerns that governments were abusing their powers in this area—not least with regard to undermining money's unique capacity to serve as a measurement of comparative value.

Measurement and Stability

The notion that universal standards of measurement existed and were in some way associated with God appears in pre-Christian Hebrew and Greek thought. Plato insisted, for instance, that God is the measure of everything, and did so in opposition to Protagoras the Sophist's claim that man is the measure of all things.[6] In Athens, it wasn't a coincidence that the standard weights and measures were dedicated to the gods and housed in the Acropolis.[7]

The Hebrew Scriptures made a fairly direct link between measures and weights and the Jewish claim that God, rather than man, was the universal measure. Proverbs, for instance, states that "A just weight and balance are the Lord's; all the weights of the bag are his work" (Prov. 16:11). Any effort therefore to falsify weights and measures was considered a very serious sin. Leviticus regarded such tampering as a direct violation of justice (Lev. 19:35–36). Deuteronomy insisted on *standard* weights and measures and specifically warned against using different measures for the same thing (Deut. 25:13–15).

Such exhortations and admonitions were especially important when it came to coinage as a reliable and standard form of measurement. Then, as now, it was understood that the absence of money that did not meet these criteria negatively impacted every sector of society. Not only did it distort the workings of prices; unreliable money also undermined the basic trust that is indispensable in any marketplace.

Against this background, it is understandable that the first extended Christian commentaries on these matters focused on maintaining the stability of the worth of a currency and condemning falsifications of currency as violations of the commandments against theft and lying. In his *De regimine principum*, for instance, Aquinas argued that

> weights and measures . . . are as necessary as the coinage for preserving the government of any lordship, since they are used in the payment of tributes, since their use decreases quarrels and projects fidelity in purchases and sales, and, finally, since they, like coins, are instruments of life and . . . imitate human action.[8]

In the premedieval and medieval world, there were two meanings to monetary stability. One was the stability of the physical integrity (mainly gold, silver, and copper) of commodity money over time. The second was the stability of the money unit's purchasing power. Aquinas was one of the first to speak about monetary stability in this sense:

> The particular virtue of currency must be that when a man presents it he immediately receives what he needs. However, it is true that currency also suffers the same as other things, viz., that it does not always obtain for a man what he wants because it cannot always be equal or of the same value. Nevertheless it ought to be so established that it retains the same value more permanently than other things.[9]

The use of the word "ought" here is revealing. Aquinas did not evidently regard monetary stability as somehow emerging automatically. It needed to be chosen and then realized as a goal.

One such choosing occurred in the eighth century, when after long periods of monetary chaos and even times in which barter arrangements prevailed, the first Holy Roman Emperor, Charlemagne, decided on a final break with the remnants of Rome's monetary system by substituting a new monetary system in place of the Roman *solidus*. Charlemagne recognized that if his empire's economy was not to sink back completely into agriculture, it needed a coinage more appropriate to its needs.[10] Thus, the state tried to assume responsibility for maintaining coinage standards, and reserved for itself the right of coinage, punishing counterfeiters severely.[11]

The State and Debasement

As the modern nation-state began emerging from the late-thirteenth century onward, rulers insisted on proclaiming their own distinctive units of account. In the fourteenth century, for instance, papal sovereignty was associated by the theologian Giles of Rome with divine power over weights and measures.[12] Such claims were used as the basis for governments to decree an exchange value on any foreign monies that managed to circulate across their territorial borders.[13]

Though some currency debasement occurred through natural wear and tear, outright fraud in the making and composition of coins by gold and silversmiths was an enormous problem in the Middle Ages. It wasn't for idle reasons that Aquinas stressed that the very word for money was derived "from *monere* [to warn], because it warns against fraud."[14] Those convicted of fraud and counterfeiting, including royal officials, were subject to punishments ranging from heavy fines to being hung, drawn, and quartered. For such offences, Jews were invariably treated far more harshly than Christians.[15]

The most significant debasers, however, were not individuals or businesses. As medieval and modern states grew, they found it increasingly difficult to live within their means. The sole right of coinage meant that rulers didn't hesitate to use coinage to serve their own ends. "Money," as Pirenne points out, "was called up or down, according as the king was creditor or debtor."[16]

In the ten years spanning the end of the thirteenth century and the beginning of the fourteenth century, for instance, French monarchs reduced the value of their currency by approximately 80 percent. At one point, the state restored the currency to its original value, only to see it devalued again during the reign of Charles IV, a ruler who not only played with the worth of the currency but also confiscated all the property of Lombard bankers in France.[17]

Debasement took many forms. One involved governments changing the ratio of different coinages: a ratio of 1 pound for 100 pennies could go to 1 pound for 120 pennies. Another was to literally dilute the currency by reducing the amount of gold in one coin and/or adulterating it with a proportion of silver. One ducat might, for instance, weigh 100 ounces of gold. You could reduce the ducat to 80 ounces of gold or take the same ducat and make it half gold and half silver. The result was to reduce the coin's metallic worth while maintaining the same face value.

There were two reasons why rulers engaged in such behavior. One was to reduce its debts. The second was to gain the profit known as *seigniorage*. To gain access to the new coinage, people had to bring in their old coinage to exchange for the new coinage, which was of a lower value. As Wood remarks, this effectively amounted to taxation without consent.[18]

Debasement as Economic Injustice

Christians were not slow to condemn these practices. The inflationary implications of currency debasement were well understood by scholastic thinkers. The French bishop William Durant the Younger (1266–1330) argued that, in addition to debilitating the coinage and undermining the common good by altering weights and measures, debasements "cause and encourage a universal rise in prices and similar kinds of fraud."[19]

The most significant early criticisms, however, were made by the French bishop and theologian Nicole Oresme of Lisieux (1320–1382) in his *Tractatus de origine natura jure et mutationibus monetarum* (1355). Oresme wrote this work in the context of intense opposition to the French government's debasement policies. By the time the longer version of the text appeared, Oresme was acting as an official advisor to a new king.

Significantly, the bishop regarded alteration of the currency as a sin worse than usury.[20] The king, he insisted, did *not* own the polity's money. He was its custodian, and his responsibility was to maintain the stability of its value.[21]

Oresme had hard words for even small debasements. In his view, it did "not avoid scandal, but begets it . . . nor is there any necessity or convenience in doing it, nor can it advantage the commonwealth."[22] The bishop saw the root cause of such debasements as the sin of greed. "I am of the opinion," he wrote, "that the main and final cause why the prince pretends to the power of altering the coinage is the profit or gain he can get from it; it would otherwise be vain to make so many and so great changes.[23]

Debasements, Oresme wrote, allowed rulers to introduce injustices in economic life—injustices that weren't likely to be immediately noticed by most of their subjects. Through debasements, he held,

> the prince could thus draw to himself almost all the money of the community and unduly impoverish his subjects. And as some chronic sicknesses are more dangerous than others because they are less perceptible, so such an exaction is the more dangerous the less obvious it is, because the oppression is less quickly felt by the people than it would be in any other form of contribution. And yet no tillage can be heavier, more general or more severe.[24]

One major injustice proceeding from currency debasements, Oresme argued, was that "money rents, yearly pensions, rates of hire and the like, cannot be well and justly taxed." Another was the manner in which debasements distorted the process of lending money and giving credit.[25] In all these situations, the possibility opened up for taxpayers and debtors to avoid paying the real amount of what they owed. Those who chose to benefit from these changes were, Oresme concluded, acting unjustly.[26]

Nor were medieval theologians slow to point out the injustices associated with governments deciding to return to a strong currency after engaging in debasements. In some instances, observed the French theologian Peter the Chanter (d. 1197), it effectively increased what people owed in debts. Many people, he stated, would be required to pay back three times as much gold or silver as the amount they had originally borrowed.[27]

Similar criticisms were articulated four hundred years later by sixteenth- and seventeenth-century scholastic thinkers. They had little doubt that one of the state's roles was to determine the community's metrical system as well as the commodity on which the mathematical and abstract unit of account was to be based. To that extent, they regarded money as a "creation" of the state. But they also maintained that any economic standard of measurement generally had to remain constant throughout time and space. Without such a measure, an indispensable prerequisite of merchant activity that could be sustained over the long term would be missing. As the Jesuit Juan de Mariana saw it,

> Weights, measures and money are . . . the foundations of commerce upon which rests the entire structure of trade. Most things are sold by weight and measure—but everything is sold by money. Everyone wants the foundations of buildings to remain firm and secure, and the same holds true for weights, measures, and money. They cannot be changed without danger and harm to commerce.[28]

Mariana knew that of which he spoke. Most of his life was lived in the Spain of King Philip II, ruler of the first global empire about which it was said the sun never set. It was also an empire at war for all but six months of Philip's reign. Taxation and the import of gold and silver from the New World were not adequate to fund the state's military commitments. The Spanish monarchy resorted to loan contracts to maintain the state's floating debt. These were not enough to stave off financial collapse. In his own lifetime, Mariana witnessed no fewer than *five* official state bankruptcies (1557, 1560, 1575, 1596, and 1607) of his native Spain—not one of which was averted by the successive currency debasements undertaken by King Philip and his successor, Philip III.

For Mariana, the central question raised by such policies was: "Can a prince in every case solve his fiscal problems on his own authority and debase his kingdom's currency by diminishing its weight or its quality?"[29] In economic terms, Mariana was attentive to the short- and long-term effects of monetary manipulation. If the supply of coins is increased, he wrote, there will be more money in the economy. This, according to Mariana, would temporarily stimulate domestic production and make money less expensive for debtors, while also allowing the king to reduce his debts.[30]

Mariana was, however, equally attentive to debasement's long-term economic costs. Such debasement would be "like giving a drink at the wrong time to a sick man. At first, it refreshes him but later aggravates the causes of his illness and increases his fever."[31] It would, for instance, result in inflationary price rises and gradually undermine commercial productivity as more people turned their attention away from innovation in the real economy and toward the wrong types of financial speculation.

More generally, however, Mariana saw currency debasement as something that benefited the government at the people's expense:

> These strategies aim at the same thing: cleaning out the pockets of the people and piling up money in the provincial treasury. Do not be taken in by the smoke and mirrors by which metal is given a greater value than it has by nature and in common estimation. Of course this does not happen without common injury. Whenever blood is let by whatever device or strategy, the body will certainly be debilitated and wasted. In the same way, a prince cannot profit without the sufferings and groans of his subjects.[32]

Rather than debase the money, Mariana suggested that fiscal order could be restored by curtailing court expenses and holding court ministers and royal officials accountable for what they spent.[33]

Money, Power, and Tyranny

However, medieval and early-modern Christian critique of monetary debasements went beyond concerns about theft and fraud on the part of secular rulers. It also touched on the limits of state power, the sources of sovereignty, and the common good.

Reflecting on such matters, the Carmelite canon lawyer and theologian Guido Terreni (c. 1270–1342) began with the premise that money was created for the common good—that of the political community and of the ruler who exercised authority over that community. It followed, he reasoned, that if rulers decided to alter the value of money in ways that benefited themselves rather than the community's common good, they became tyrants.[34] The theme of tyranny also figured in the thoughts of the Dominican bishop and canonist Peter de la Palu (1275–1342) on this matter. "If a king alters money for his own utility and to the detriment of his subjects," the bishop stated, "he is a tyrant rather than a king." The tyranny lay in promoting personal interest over the common good.[35]

Oresme's view was similar. "Money," he insisted, "is essentially established and devised for the good of the community. And since the prince is the most public person [*personam publicam*] and of the highest authority, it follows that he should make money for the community and stamp it with a suitable design."[36] That, however, did not mean that the ruler "owned" the community's money. According to Oresme, "money is a balancing instrument for the exchange of natural wealth. . . . It is therefore the property of those who possess such wealth. For if a man gives bread or bodily labor in exchange for money, the money he receives is his as much as the bread or bodily labor of which he . . . was free to dispose."[37]

For this reason, Oresme even questioned state monopolies of the money supply:

> But if anyone should say that . . . certain commodities are the private property of the prince for which he may set his own prices, as some say is the case with salt and *a fortiori* with money, we answer that a monopoly or *gabelle* of salt, or any

other necessity, is unjust. And that princes who have made laws to give themselves this privilege are the men of whom the Lord says, in the words of the prophet Isaiah: "Woe unto them that decree unrighteous decrees, and write grievousness which they have prescribed" [Isa. 10:1] . . . money is the property of the commonwealth.[38]

The political implications of these and similar claims were enormous. Figures such as Oresme effectively concluded that only the body politic—rather than the ruler acting alone—could decide if and when coinage needed to change or be debased, even in emergencies.[39] Rulers simply could not, Oresme specified, make decisions about such matters on their own whim.[40]

Here we should note that medieval theologians did not maintain that reducing the value of a currency or monetary unit was unthinkable. There *were* instances, they believed, in which a just ruler could alter the coinage's value *if* the kingdom's common good demanded it and *if* other ways of raising money were more harmful to society. Aquinas, for instance, maintained that there were conditions in which governments could alter the coinage. Yet he warned they should be very cautious in doing so "because this results in harm to the people, since it is a measure of things, and therefore to alter money or coin amounts to the same thing as altering a pair of scales or any kind of weight."[41]

There is considerable evidence that rulers and communities were influenced by these ideas. By the 1300s, French bishops were asking the king to consult them and the nobles before making decisions about the coinage. Across the Channel, the English Parliament insisted in 1311 that the political community rather than the king owned the nation's money. Parliamentary approval was consequently needed to approve any alteration. Though currency debasements were sometimes authorized because of a shortage of bullion, it had to be done with parliamentary consent.[42]

Mariana voiced many of the same arguments as his medieval predecessors but in sharper terms. He placed the wrongness of rulers debasing currency without their subjects' approval in the same category as taxation without consent. "The private goods," he insisted, "are not at the disposal of the king. Thus, he must not take all or part of them without the approval of those who have the right to them."[43] Central to Mariana's position was his claim that since the prince "is not the master of the private possessions of his subjects, he will not be able to take away arbitrarily any part of their possessions for this or any other reason or ploy. Such seizure occurs whenever money is debased."[44] The king, Mariana held, "is not empowered to levy taxes on unwilling subjects and cannot set up monopolies for merchandise; he is not empowered to make fresh profit from debased money."[45]

Mariana was prepared to allow the monarch to alter the currency's value without the people's consent only in very specific circumstances, and provided that two conditions were met: "we grant the king the authority to debase money without the people's consent in the pressing circumstances of war or siege—provided that the debasement is not extended beyond the time of need and that, when peace has been restored, he faithfully makes satisfaction to those who suffered loss."[46]

Debt, Bonds, and Public Finances

Debasement wasn't the only way in which governments sought to address their financial challenges. One feature of the medieval period was the gradual emergence of what we would recognize today as bonds and bond markets.

These financial instruments first developed and acquired sophistication in northern Italy's commercial republics. In the thirteenth century, as part of an effort to fund the costs of war and public administration, the Venetian Republic issued a decree permitting the government to spend up to 3,000 lires a month to fund its ordinary needs, with any spending beyond that to be used to (1) pay for the costs of war, (2) pay down the state's debts, and, crucially, (3) pay 5 percent interest to those from whom the government had borrowed money.

This innovation had several effects. The first was to facilitate the gathering together of all previous loans to the state into one pool. A second was to devote part of the state's revenue to paying interest. The third was to guarantee all who lent money to the state 5 percent interest per year.[47] As time went on, the capital raised from such loans was used for other purposes, ranging from maintaining legal systems to investments in infrastructure.[48]

For lenders, there were significant drawbacks to these arrangements. Most such loans to governments were involuntary, because of the typically bad credit of governments. Furthermore, government-guaranteed interest-rate payments were generally below market rate.[49] Loans were given to a government fund in the form of what were called *mons* (because of mountain-sized debts). Lenders to *mons* were given a share that paid a fixed rate of interest and that was redeemable at the option.[50] Though actual redemptions were irregular at best, the debt balance of most states grew enormously.[51]

It wasn't just secular rulers who embraced such methods for managing public finances. The papacy itself followed the pattern of other European states by regularizing the funding of its public debts through the establishment of the *Monte della fede* in 1526, followed by over forty more such funds over the next one hundred years. These were managed by a group of private bankers who provided most of the loans to the papacy. In return, they were given control of specific revenues.[52]

These changes to public finances in medieval and early modern Europe provided the basis for particular innovations in emerging capital markets. It did not take long for the shares in *mons*, for instance, to become objects of trade.[53] What was traded was not simply the title to the principal but also the interest claims and any arrears in interest payments owed by the state to the holder of the bond.[54] Their price reflected interest rates as well as the degree of confidence in the issuing state's fiscal well-being. As the size of a state's official debt grew, the share price dropped.[55]

By the late-thirteenth century, Venice and Genoa had transformed their floating debts into one consolidated public debt managed by a government office. This allowed the easier trading of bonds on open capital markets. Holders of government debts used them as collateral, sold them, and even gave them away as dowries! Initially it was forbidden to trade these bonds outside the issuing state's borders. Eventually, however, foreigners were allowed to buy and trade government debt.[56] Crucial in this connection was the confidence that governments would not, for reasons of expediency, retroactively interfere with the transactions of those who traded debt.

The not-infrequent inability of governments to pay interest on such debt meant that those who traded and purchased these shares were, to an extent, engaged in speculation on open markets concerning interest payments and likely rates of interest over time. A market consequently emerged on the basis of estimating the future trend of prices for shares in *mons* along with options on credit for a set price at a future date.

Not surprisingly, the question arose as to whether these practices constituted usury. After all, to purchase a share in a *mons* involved not just the purchase of a government debt but also the interest on that debt. Franciscan theologians such as Francis of Empoli (d. 1347) were at the forefront of defending these practices. As early as 1310, some theologians argued that they were licit because it was the sale not of money per se but of a right to a sale of money and subsequent payments.[57] It was thus a true sale of a *real* obligation in which the new owner assumed all the potential of loss and gain.

The most extensive defense, however, of trading entitlements to interest on loans to governments was mounted by the canon lawyer Laurentius de Ridolfis (1360–1442). In his treatise on usury, he noted, first, that the origins of these loans more often than not lay in compulsion by the state. The lender was not therefore intending or choosing anything. Second, because the interest rate was usually low, Ridolfis maintained, no one could be said to be making a profit. Third, these forced loans resulted in people being deprived of their capital; the bondholders should therefore be compensated for the foregone gain (*lucrum cessans*).[58] Moreover, Ridolfis suggested that these loans were preferable to the state simply taking what it needed from wealthy citizens without going through the formal process of requesting a loan with some promise of compensation. Outright confiscations of money and capital, Ridolfis reasoned, would require

the use of violence and most likely breed sedition against the government.[59]

Bankers and Princes

Bonds and government debt were not the only ways in which medieval and early-modern states addressed their financial challenges.
They turned out to be very successful in incorporating private banks
and bankers into their financial arrangements—a practice that, in
many instances, attracted criticism from Christian theologians.

The greater availability of capital in the conditions of the Commercial Revolution meant that rulers were able to frequently borrow
money to pursue particular projects, especially those that they considered unlikely to be funded by taxes. As early as the twelfth century,
rulers began institutionalizing the process. They established regular
relationships with specific Christian and Jewish moneylenders, often
in the face of considerable disapproval of particular church authorities, who regarded this as government-sanctioned usury.[60]

As these relationships became more established, bankers were able
to introduce some regularity to royal finances in countries such as
France and England, not least by smoothing out the highs and lows
of royal revenues.[61] Bankers would typically take as security for such
loans crown or princely jewels and other symbols of sovereignty.[62]
This symbolized the integration of private and public finances.

The papacy exemplified the intermeshing of government and private finance in the medieval and early-modern period. Up until the
fourteenth century, the papacy deposited and borrowed modest sums
with Italian merchant bankers.[63] But the papacy was also the recipient
of large revenues, and unequipped to deal with the management of
the income and its subsequent dispersal throughout medieval Christendom. The popes subsequently turned to Italian bankers, initially
from Siena but eventually from Florence, to manage their finances.
These banks provided the usual deposit, loan, and transfer services.
They also, however, took increasing responsibility for collecting
many ecclesiastical taxes and managing the complicated process of

transferring funds around the church's various institutions through-out Europe.[64] One reason why the French city of Avignon became a major center of finance, international credit, and money exchanges was the papacy's transfer to Avignon in 1305 and the establishment of bankers around the papal court.

The degree of closeness of bankers to rulers varied from country to country. In France, for instance, some banks were practically incor-porated into the machinery of state as professional administrators of public finances and collectors of customs levies. By contrast, bankers were used by the government in England on a regular basis, but kept at one remove from official state business.[65]

Regardless of its precise form, involvement in government finance created serious dilemmas for bankers. To do business in the medieval and early-modern world, bankers needed the protection of rulers. Yet the potential for trouble was significant. Bankers were placed in invidious positions whenever, for instance, different rulers to whom they were lending went to war with each other.[66] When governments grew dissatisfied with the particular banking arrangements into which they had entered, they would often act against bankers, confis-cate their property, sometimes imprison them, and occasionally force banks to renegotiate loans on terms more favorable to the monarch.[67] In the case of Jewish financiers, rulers didn't hesitate to remove their implied protection whenever politically or economically convenient to do so, such as when Edward I expelled the entire Jewish popula-tion of England in 1290.[68]

The other problem was the ever-present risk of repudiation of debt by the state, and the inability of banks to do much about it. This happened regularly to Italian and German bankers. In the fourteenth century, a wave of defaults by rulers across Europe ranging from Tus-cany to England and the forced rescheduling of interest payments in France bankrupted many private financial institutions.[69]

These bankruptcies occurred not simply because rulers wouldn't make payments and banks had overextended their credit involve-ment in government finance.[70] Many banks were so involved in the financial arrangements of so many rulers that one serious default could easily set off a chain reaction. In such instances, banks were unable to recover their loans and proved incapable of transferring amounts quickly enough throughout Europe in order to meet their obligations.[71]

It is, however, revealing that a financial crisis of this scale happened only once in the history of medieval and early-modern banking. Some have speculated that the extent of the fourteenth-century bankruptcies made such an impression on Italian banks' collective memory that they were determined never to repeat the same mistakes. They subsequently became extremely organized among themselves in how they managed their business with governments. Banks would enter into contracts with rulers and then divide the contracts into shares. These in turn could be purchased by bankers from various places. The effect was to pool and thereby reduce the risk of exposure. As a consequence, although bankruptcies continued to occur, there was nothing like the overexposure and chain reaction effect that engulfed European banks in the mid-fourteenth century.[72]

Governments also had no wish to repeat such an experience and started to manage their finances more directly and in more sophisticated ways. This involved developing new institutional structures for managing their debt.[73] One of the first "public" banks, established in 1401 as a semi-official agent of the state, was the *Taula de Canvi de Barcelona*. This preceded the most famous northern European bank, the Bank of Amsterdam, by 208 years. As well as acting as fiscal agent for Barcelona and Catalonia, it was authorized to make loans to the city of Barcelona for the redemption of outstanding annuities and paying down of government debt. It was not a central bank, not least because it was forbidden from entering into interbank loans with private banks.[74] It did, however, compete with private banks and accept deposits from them. It lasted until 1835 when it was absorbed into the Bank of Spain.

Against Monopolies

Despite the risks associated with involvement in public finances, many bankers evidently considered them to be risks worth running. One reason was that rulers guaranteed them some protection in a world in which bankers were suspected and often resented, especially if they were foreigners or Jews. Over time, relationships with kings even created the possibility for bankers to ascend into government service and receive gifts and preferment from those and from other rulers.[75]

A second reason was that the profits for banks involved in bolstering and managing public finances were considerable. Many merchants even moved away from trade and private loans toward more or less dealing exclusively with state finance.[76] It was not just large international banks but also smaller ones who engaged in this business.[77] Of all the liquid capital available in medieval and early-modern Europe, it seems that the greatest amount went to the state.[78] By the late-medieval period, many banks were practically involved full-time in supporting public finances and paid steadily decreasing attention to the private economy.

A third reason for bankers' appetite for involvement in public finance was that, in return for loans, backing the public debt, and managing government finances, rulers would often grant banks lucrative privileges and monopolies that promised them more immediate income and less need to compete for private business. Control of tax revenues in return for loans to rulers seemed to many bankers like a good long-term tradeoff.[79] Much of the business of banks was focused on gaining monopoly positions on anything ranging from mining to the wool trade.[80] In many cases, bankers took over the very business of minting money and the associated work of mining for precious minerals as different rulers sought to establish their own monetary systems to underscore their sovereignty.[81] The most prominent example was the Fugger banking family. It was granted control of the entire output of copper mines in Hungary and the Tyrol by Emperor Maximilian.[82]

Such arrangements, however, drew significant criticism from Christian thinkers. Though theologians and canonists were generally cautious about commenting on the involvement of banks in public finances (including the papacy's finances), they were skeptical of the development of monopoly control over any one trade or industry.

While Adam Smith is often seen as the great opponent of monopoly, the Codex of Roman law had long embodied laws against monopolies and illicit pacts among merchants.[83] Christian opposition to monopolies flowed from the principle that the just price is normally the *market* price. State-sanctioned monopolies enhanced the price of a good or service beyond what it would otherwise receive in the marketplace. Monopoly generally thus violated justice as well as basic injunctions against charity.

Canon law treated monopoly profits as ill-gotten profits.[84] While willing to make exceptions for emergency situations, theologians such as Antoninus of Florence and Bernadine of Siena argued against the formation of any temporary or permanent cartels in any industry for the purpose of securing higher prices and larger profits, not least because this hurt the poor.[85] Early modern Catholic theologians such as Lessius were especially critical of monopolies established by legal grants from rulers, portraying them as sins against justice and charity.[86] Protestant theologians such as the Calvinist Johannes Althusius agreed. If anything, they were even more outspoken in their condemnation of monopolies.[87] To this extent, Christian theologians put themselves firmly against the trend to state-supervised mercantilism and cartels in the banking industry.

An Uncultivated Part of the Vineyard

After the mid-seventeenth century, it becomes difficult to find extended Christian treatments of public finance. This reflects a broader pattern of relative neglect of financial questions on the part of Christians. In fact, the truth is, as de Lauzun notes, that the in-depth study of private and public financial issues by Christians experienced a "long eclipse" from the late-seventeenth century onward.[88] Even financial collapses with as far-reaching political and economic effects such as the South Sea Bubble and Mississippi Bubble in the early-eighteenth century didn't elicit much commentary from church authorities or theologians at the time. The reasons for this relative dearth of commentary are not hard to discern. First, the usury issues had been largely resolved. Second, scholarship and universities began a process of secularization and specialization during the late-seventeenth century. The study of economic questions gradually became separated from the realms of ethics and theology. A third factor was the systematic critique launched by many Enlightenment thinkers of Christianity's most basic claims. Christianity's best minds shifted their attention away from issues such as the morality of charging interest to defending core Christian dogmas and doctrines. Third, when Christians began to regain their economic voice, they found themselves having to address the many new things produced in the wake of the Industrial Revolution. Specific attention to money and finance per se was in these circumstances a low priority compared to the necessity of responding to the rise of liberalism, socialism, and communism, not to mention the social and economic upheavals associated with industrialization, or what nineteenth-century Christians called "the social question."

As industrial capitalism took hold of Europe and North America, Christians did not remain silent about finance. With a few notable exceptions, however, the subject was not a feature of their analysis of socio-economic issues. Far more attention was devoted in Christian social ethics to new issues such as the role of unions, the state's responsibilities in industrial economies, property and its limits, poverty, and the requirements of justice and charity in modern capitalist societies. Also absent throughout much of this period in virtually all schools of Christian reflection on economics was a conceptual framework specifically geared to help Christians think about and contribute to the correct ordering of finance.

One lesson of the 2008 financial crisis is that its roots were surely more than just economic. In his 2010 address to Britain's political and cultural leaders in London's Westminster Hall, Benedict XVI suggested that "the lack of a solid ethical foundation for economic activity has contributed to the grave difficulties now being experienced by millions of people throughout the world."[89] It is also true, however, that specifically Christian outlines of a framework that allows Christians to think *cum ecclesia* (with the church) about finance are scarce. Compared to the quite detailed treatment given by modern

Christian social commentary to subjects such as the determination of wages, finance continues to be a poor relation. Given the pivotal role now played by finance in the global economy, the urgency of outlining such a framework and then applying it to some of the pressing issues of our time is more necessary than ever.

Further Reading

Day, John. *Money and Finance in the Age of Merchant Capitalism.* Oxford: Blackwell, 1999.

Goetzmann, William N., and K. Geert Rouwenhorst (eds.). *The Origins of Value: The Financial Innovations That Created Modern Capital Markets.* Oxford: Oxford University Press, 2005.

Goldthwaite, Richard A. *The Economy of Renaissance Florence.* Baltimore: Johns Hopkins University Press, 2009.

Mariana, Juan de, S.J. "A Treatise on the Alteration of Money." Translated by Patrick T. Brannan, S.J. Pages 247–327 in Stephen Grabill (ed.), *Sourcebook in Late-Scholastic Monetary Theory.* Lanham, MD: Lexington Books, 2007.

Oresme, Nicholas. *The De moneta of Nicholas Oresme and English Mint Documents* (1355). Translated by Charles Johnson. London: Thomas Nelson & Sons, 1956.

PART II

Theory

5

Freedom, Flourishing, and Justice

Wisdom is a precious legacy, a boon for those on whom the sun shines. For as money gives protection, so does wisdom.

Ecclesiastes 7:12

What good is money in a foolish hand? To purchase wisdom, when he has no sense?

Proverbs 17:16

Throughout the Bible, reflections on money invariably go hand in hand with discussions of the nature of wisdom and foolishness. Scripture's understanding of wisdom does not amount to exhortations to be pragmatic, let alone utilitarian. Instead wisdom is associated with a person's search for the truth and then, in light of knowledge of this truth, freely choosing to living in that truth—including the truth about good and evil. As Deuteronomy famously states, "I set before you life or death. Choose life, then, so that you and your descendants may live" (Deut. 30:19). Elevating the pursuit of wealth over love of God is one of the paths that Christianity has always insisted leads toward death—understood as the free choice to separate oneself eternally from Christ, which Christianity calls hell.

Early in his pontificate Pope Francis stressed the foolishness of excessive attachment to wealth by observing that there's something profoundly irrational about "greed for money that you can't take with you and have to leave" when you die.[1] The problem, it should be reiterated, is not the possession of money itself. As no less than St. Thomas More once observed, "It is not a sin to have riches, but to love riches." For Christians, the question is how we integrate the possession and use of money into our life *as* Christians, and, second, how money can serve the common good of all the communities in which we live, move, and have our being.

A similar approach lies at the heart of the development of an authentically Christian understanding of the proper orientation and ends of finance. The final goal for every Christian is beyond this world: it lies in the hope we have of oneness with Christ at the end of time and on the day of judgment. Living out that hope in this world and thereby contributing to building up the Kingdom of God that is already mysteriously present in certain respects in the here and now requires Christians to reflect seriously on how finance and our financial systems promote the all-around flourishing of each person and every community instead of its opposite: disintegration as persons, the dissolution of community, and ultimately despair.

Our survey of the long history of the Christian analysis of finance illustrates that Christians certainly brought to bear various principles—commutative justice, concern for the poor, a concern to limit the state's power to act arbitrarily, to name just a few—on issues associated with finance. The theological and moral settings from which these principles are derived, however, were rarely spelled out, perhaps because the authors presumed that their Christian and mostly scholarly audiences knew and accepted this assumed background.

That same assumption often seems operative today. The Note on reforming the international finance system produced in 2011 by the Pontifical Council for Justice and Peace, for instance, limited its consideration of the theological and moral framework that should inform Christian reflection on finance to one short paragraph, entitled "Presupposition."[2] This referenced the responsibility of Christians to contribute to the common good. The Note then immediately proceeded to outline a long interpretation of the development of the post-1945 financial system that could have easily been written by someone with little or no interest in Christianity.

What follows is an effort to spell out Christian principles for thinking through the ends and nature of finance. The starting point for this reflection is how Christianity understands the nature of human flourishing and, critically, how this relates to the common good. We then consider what this means for the use and ownership of material things, its implications for wealth, and how it affects the Christian understanding of the nature of justice.

Doing Good, Avoiding Evil, and Human Flourishing

The idea of human flourishing is as old as Aristotle. Christianity, however, has a quite specific conception of what this means. From the beginning of Christ's ministry, human flourishing is understood in terms of each person's liberation *from* sin and his free submission *to* Jesus Christ as the one who sets us free. "For freedom," Paul proclaims, "Christ set us free; so stand firm and do not submit again to the yoke of slavery" (Gal. 5:1).[3]

Human freedom and human flourishing are thus not just associated with each other; they are intimately connected with doing good and avoiding evil. Saint Augustine put it this way in his most famous book, *The City of God*: "the good man, although he is a slave, is free; but the bad man, even if he reigns, is a slave, and that not of one man, but, what is far more grievous, of as many masters as he has vices."[4]

The inevitable subsequent question is how do we do good and avoid evil in the various conditions in which we find ourselves. Many answers provided by the Christian faith are to be found in revelation, most notably the Decalogue. Not only are the Ten Commandments referred to more times in the New Testament than in the whole of the Hebrew scriptures, but they are also the one element of the law inherited from the Jewish people that is still valid in the New Covenant inaugurated by Christ's life, death, and resurrection.[5]

But perhaps the most significant contribution made by Christ himself, Paul, and numerous Church Fathers was to present the

Decalogue as a manifestation of God's sovereignty in *creation itself*. In his famous conversation with the rich young man (Matt. 19:16–19; Mark 10:17–19; Luke 18:18–20), Christ reaffirms the Decalogue—most notably, the second tablet of the thou-shalt-nots—and radicalizes its precepts in the Sermon on the Mount (Matt. 5:17–28). Likewise Paul stresses that the precepts of the commandments are written on the heart: that is, *into* human nature itself (Rom. 1:23–31; 2:14–15; 13:8–10). This means that they can be understood and lived by anyone by virtue of our possession of reason and free will.

The Christian vision of the good life, of human flourishing, isn't therefore about doing whatever we "happen" to will or just feel like. It involves, first, consistently choosing *not* to do evil, and then just as consistently choosing the good. Christian liberty and the Christian life cannot be equated with license: that is, a liberty detached from revelation and each person's natural capacity for reason. Through the knowledge that comes through faith in Christ—a knowledge that surpasses but which is consistent with the insights of natural human reason—Christians can know the truth about themselves and good and evil, and freely orientate their wills so that they avoid evil and integrate the good into their lives through their free choices and actions.

So how does a human being flourish?[6] The argument of Christians ranging from Augustine to Aquinas is that we do so *in the process of free choice*. When we freely choose fundamental goods such as life and health, friendship, knowledge, integrity, beauty, and work, we literally integrate them into our identity through our deliberation, choices, and actions. These choices about ourselves *last* until they are negated by a contrary choice. Understood in this way, we human beings are truly *self*-determining and *self*-determined beings. We thus become the substance of our free choices. Aquinas provides what is perhaps the most concise description of this process of "becoming":

> Action is of two sorts: one sort—action [*actio*] in a strict sense—issues from the agent into something external to change it . . . the other sort—properly called activity [*operatio*]—does not

issue into something external but remains within the agent itself perfecting it.[7]

In late 2012, Benedict XVI summed up this Christian understanding of freedom and human flourishing in a beautiful reflection on the Ten Commandments:

> God has given us the Commandments to educate us to liberty and genuine love, so that we can be truly happy. They are a sign of the love of God the Father, of his desire to teach us the correct discernment of good and evil, of the true and the false, of the just and the unjust. They are comprehensible to all precisely because they establish the fundamental values in concrete norms and rules; in putting them into practice man can walk on the path of *true liberty*, which renders him firm in the way that leads him to *life* and *happiness*.[8]

It's worth underscoring here that there are countless paths toward freely realizing the one goal of human flourishing. The precise way in which even quite similar people realize any number of fundamental goods in their lives is often quite different. Yet none of this implies we cannot say *one* kind of choice is always good while *another* is always evil. Worshiping the one true God is *always* meritorious. Theft is *always* sinful.

Sociability and the Common Good

While the act of free choice to follow Christ and live out his commandments is ultimately one that can only be carried out by individuals, humans are also innately interdependent beings. All of us need others to flourish. No child can raise itself. No banker can grow his business without customers and employees. Just as it is impossible to know Christ and the scriptures without the witness of the body of Christ that we call the church, all of us are reliant on others if we are to have any chance of flourishing.

Certain conditions also need to prevail within any community, be it a school or a nation, if people are to have the opportunity to flourish. Choosing the good and avoiding evil is obviously not impossible in conditions of anarchy. But it is far more difficult than in those societies where the rule of law prevails.

The conditions that help people to flourish under their own volition are known in Christian teaching as the "common good." In 1965, the Fathers of the Second Vatican Council summed up centuries of Christian reflection on the common good by describing it as "the sum of those conditions of the social life whereby men, families and associations more adequately and readily may attain their own perfection."[9]

The words "attain their own perfection" are especially important. First, they describe the goal of the common good: human flourishing. Second, they underscore that the advancement of the common good is about assisting all individuals and communities to realize their flourishing. It is *not* about seeking to realize it "on their behalf." Unless persons and communities *freely choose* moral and spiritual goods through their actions, they cannot be said to be truly participating in these goods.

Discerning the particular responsibilities of any community with regard to the common good is a far from simple affair. Take, for instance, the political community and its legitimate authorities, which we call the government. A government that sought to predetermine all of our decisions would severely limit our scope for free choice. At the same time, Christianity has always insisted that governments do have a role in shaping the moral culture. Summarizing this teaching, Archbishop Charles Chaput once commented:

> The ultimate goal of our laws is to make us morally good. Our laws should help us accord with the design God has written into human nature. Thus, [Jacques] Maritain writes, civil law "should always maintain a general orientation toward virtuous life, and make the common behavior tend, at each level, to the full accomplishment of moral law."[10]

We also know that the absence of certain conditions that rely heavily on the state for their effectiveness can make human flourishing more difficult to realize.[11] Rule of law, for instance, is impossible without government institutions.

Further complicating matters is a fact that Judaism and Christianity have consistently affirmed from the beginning of God's revelation of himself to humanity: the reality of *sin*. Christians believe that Christ saved each of us from the first sin of our parents. At the same time, the effects of original sin remain everywhere. Even saints have misused their freedom at different points of their lives and sinned.

This particular insight means that while we all strive to attain holiness, it is a folly to think that heaven can be realized on earth. Neither the economy writ large nor the financial sector is somehow immune from the demands of justice. Yet Christians should be wary of the ever-present temptation to imagine that the fullness of justice, which Christ will deliver at the end of time, can somehow be realized in the here and now, whether in the legal system, politics, or the economy. The briefest glance at twentieth-century history reminds us that such utopian agendas invariably produce suffering and injustice.

Material Goods: Common Use and Private Ownership

Beyond our need for other people and communities, humans also require what might be called "instrumental goods" in order to flourish. These are goods that have their own value and that can be used to facilitate the pursuance of fundamental goods, but that are not in themselves fulfilling. The most obvious of such goods is the created world, of which human beings are part (since they too are created by God), but over which human beings have been charged with a type of authority. Much of the first three chapters of the book of Genesis details how humans exercise a genuine "lordship" over all other created things, albeit a dominion that is not absolute. The human being is indeed the apex of the created world brought into existence by God. We are not, however, above the law of God. In this sense, our dominion is one of stewardship: a stewardship that gives direction to what we can choose and for which each of us will have to render an account to God at the end of our lives.

Money is a prominent example of such an instrumental good. It's not a fundamental good in the sense that goods such as life, truth, and friendship are intrinsic to human persons and communities. Rather money is a good that derives its intelligibility to humans as a means of helping us to participate in fundamental goods. Through money, a husband and wife are able to obtain any number of other goods and services that help them to live out their marriage and provide for their children. Likewise money in the form of capital enables entrepreneurs to build businesses that grow and employ people, thereby enabling others to participate in the good of work.

Problems invariably begin whenever people start to view money (or any other instrumental good) as an ultimate good, or when fundamental goods are subordinated to the pursuit of money (or any other instrumental good). While each instrumental good produced through human minds and work has its own value, it does not last. Such goods eventually corrode, malfunction, or find themselves being consumed, replaced, superseded, or rendered obsolete. Eventually they disappear from our lives when we die.

These limitations should not, however, distract us from the fact that money and other instrumental goods are crucial elements for the promotion of human flourishing. So how then do we ensure that our use of instrumental goods such as money accords with the demands of human flourishing? Part of the traditional Christian answer to that question is to be found in what is called the "universal destination of material goods."

The origins of this idea lie in the principle that God has given the earth and all it contains to be used by and on behalf of *all* people.[12] In the beginning and now, God provides material goods for the use of all. The question then becomes one of *how* this common use is to be realized. The Christian response has been that it is usually realized (though not strictly) through private ownership—so much so that private possession of property isn't just licit, but usually necessary for realizing this goal. The commandment against theft can be understood at least partly pointing in this direction.

In his *Summa theologiae*, Aquinas outlined three basic reasons in favor of the private ownership of economic goods. First, he notes, people tend to take better care of what is theirs than of what is common to everyone, since individuals tend to shirk responsibilities that belong to nobody in particular. Second, if everyone were responsible for everything, the result would be confusion. Third, dividing up things generally produces a more peaceful state of affairs; by contrast, sharing things in common often results in tension. Individual ownership, then—understood as the power to manage and dispose of things—is legitimate.[13]

Yet Christianity doesn't regard private ownership of material goods as absolute. In the first place, private ownership is a *means* of ensuring common use and that material goods serve human beings. Aquinas himself specified that "if the need be so manifest and urgent that it is evident that the present need must be remedied by whatever means be at hand (for instance when a person is in some imminent danger, and there is no other possible remedy), then it is lawful for a man to succor his own need by means of another's property."[14] Elsewhere Aquinas provides a clearer indication of what constitutes "imminent danger." In discussing almsgiving, he states that "it is not every sort of need that binds us as a matter of strict obligation, but only what is a matter of life and death. This is where Ambrose's dictum applies, 'Feed the man who is dying. Refuse, and you kill him.'"[15]

Later thinkers working within the orthodox Christian tradition reflect a broad continuation of Aquinas's treatment of this subject. That said, different dimensions of this teaching were stressed more than others. One sees more extensive critiques of common ownership in later scholastic writings. The Dominican theologian Domingo de Soto (1494–1560) repeated Aquinas's criticism of common ownership, but also stressed other particular negative features. Common ownership, he maintained, tended to corrode the virtue of liberality, not least because "those who own nothing cannot be liberal."[16] Mercado noted that people tend to be more naturally inclined to care for their homes rather than the state. "If universal love," he wrote, "will not induce people to take care of their things, then private interest will. Hence private goods will multiply. Had they remained in common possession, the opposite will be true."[17] Other scholastics, such as Mariana, underlined the abuses associated with common ownership. Speaking of his own religious order (the Jesuits), he exclaimed, "Certainly it is natural for people to spend much more when they are supplied in common than when they have to obtain things on their own. The extent of our common expenses is unbelievable!"[18]

A second condition that Christianity has attached to private property is that the private nature of our property does not mean we are justified in using it exclusively for ourselves, especially in the face of others' authentic needs. Private property is not an end in itself. It is *for* something. Christianity therefore not only insists that we should use our "surplus goods" (what people have left over once they have used their property to meet their own and their families' needs) to assist others, but that we should be ready to use our essential wealth to serve others. Saints ranging from Basil to Lactantius, Augustine, Gregory the Great, Bonaventure, Albert the Great, Ambrose, and Aquinas are crystal clear about this.[19]

Surplus and Essential Wealth

A number of qualifications need to be made here. First, the precise distinction between essential and surplus property is not exactly the same for every person. Much depends, for instance, upon a person's vocation in life. The owner of a large company may have much wealth at his disposal, but very little of it may actually be surplus wealth after he has met his obligations to his family, his employees, and his customers, not to mention maintaining the level of capital in his business that enables it to stay alive, let alone grow.

In his book *What Your Money Means* (2008), the businessman, financier, and philanthropist Frank Hanna outlines helpful criteria that enable anyone—whatever the profession—to distinguish between essential and surplus wealth. He suggests that essential wealth consists of what is needed to pay for (1) our own bare necessities, (2) our own genuine needs, (3) our own profession-based needs, (4) the bare necessities of those who depend on me, (5) the genuine needs of those who depend on us, and (6) what he calls beneficial goods for ourselves and for those who depend on us.

Beneficial goods, Hanna argues, are those that "improve the life and character of the person who benefits from them; they leave us better equipped to do the good things we're called to do."[20] In short, it's a question of vocation. An example would be a business executive who pays for a year of foreign language training at a foreign language school in order to improve his ability to operate in business at the international level. Certainly, beneficial goods are on the borderline between essential and surplus wealth. We may, Hanna writes, still have enough wealth if we can't pay for beneficial goods, Still, he says, it is better if we possess the resources to pay for such goods insofar as they facilitate the flourishing of ourselves and our dependants.

So what is surplus wealth? It is, Hanna states, "money that's not demanded in any way by the obligations inherent in our circumstances and state in life."[21] *This* is the wealth that all of us have the immediate responsibility to direct toward the common good. That doesn't mean that we are somehow required to hand it all over to the government or simply give it away willy-nilly. The responsibility to use our nonsurplus wealth remains, for the most part, ours. But it does mean that Christians should be deploying this segment of their wealth to aid the flourishing of the less fortunate.

The principle of common use and the universal destination of material goods should not be understood as a type of final state of affairs in which a perfect distribution of material wealth is achieved once and for all and never changes. This would be to deny the truth of human freedom and the fact that people's responsibilities, obligations, and holdings of wealth are in a constant state of flux. What matters is that we put our wealth to work so that the conditions that promote the flourishing of every person and each community are enhanced.

Finance's Ultimate Legitimacy

From a Christian standpoint, the genius of private property is the manner in which it gives individuals and communities the capacity to mobilize their wealth in ways that promote the common good and the principle of common use. Some of this wealth consists of natural and manufactured products. At the same time, wealth can also be actualized in the form of capital in certain economic conditions. Some of this should certainly be used by Christians for charitable purposes—almsgiving being a constant exhortation for Christians. But another way of deploying such wealth is through *investment*. As noted in Chapter 3, the emergence of relatively mobile forms of investment capital was crucial for the development of the first forms of capitalism in the medieval period.

Herein lies the fundamental legitimacy for modern financial systems. Insofar as they help to facilitate the allocation of resources among individuals, households, entrepreneurs, businesses, and governments, financial systems can help us to realize the principle of common use in ways that respect private ownership on a national and international scale. Through private finance, anyone can invest surplus capital in investment firms that place capital in businesses whose work helps to spur economic development in numerous parts of the world at the very same time. That same person can also invest some of his essential and surplus capital in a retirement fund that's designed to help pay for his retirement. Likewise the financial system allows government institutions, first, to issue bonds that attract some people's capital, and, second, to use the capital raised through bond issues to invest in projects that enable government to make contributions to the common good that are beyond the capacity of private actors, such as public works and national defense.

On a broader scale, financial systems also create efficiencies in the investment and deployment of capital by individuals, businesses, and governments that, while certainly designed to produce profit, also potentially promote a better stewardship of available capital resources, which might otherwise be wasted. As we will see, this is one of the essential roles of speculation. Another important function is the way that modern finance enables (again, at least potentially) a better management of risk in ways that increase potential gains (and perhaps even distribute them to wider segments of the population) and reduce potential losses.

Financial systems also introduce more flexibility and freedom into how people match the actual and potential capital at their disposal with what they need and value at different points of time. In terms of formal economics, this is referred to as "intertemporal choice." This involves assessing the relative value that people assign to two or more potential payoffs at varying points in time in light of the known and unknown trade-offs of given choices. For our purposes, the point is that the enhanced potential that finance provides to borrow, lend, and invest over time allows different people to exercise potentially more control over, for instance, *when* they choose to buy a house, acquire higher education, retire, or begin and expand a business. To that extent, the scope for a person's flourishing can be widened.

The word "potential" features significantly in the preceding paragraphs. Financial systems throughout the world are not uniform. And none are perfect. On one level, this reflects the fact that financial systems ultimately consist of fallible sinful human beings and reflect millions of daily choices by those very same fallible sinful human beings. Some of these choices—whether by individuals acting on their own behalf or in the form of a financial firm's decisions—will be based on imprudent and often reckless assessments of risk. Other financial actors will choose to commit wrongs such as fraud. And even if an action involves no choice or even an intention to do wrong, there will always be side effects: some beneficial, some not so beneficial, some foreseeable, and some unforeseeable. To a certain extent, financial systems can minimize the effects of imprudent and wrong choices as well as negative side effects. There are, however, many instances in which the same system can magnify the negative impact of such choices far beyond what even the best financial analysts anticipate.

It is also the case that all financial systems embody, at different levels and to varying degrees, various dysfunctionalities, none of which may have been intended but which have nevertheless assumed concrete form. An example of such dysfunctionality might be distorted incentives that encourage people to borrow what they are unlikely to be able to pay back. Then there are the limitations of financial systems that reflect our innate limits as human beings. This is manifested, for instance, in the fact that even advanced economic forecasting, upon which central banks often make interest-rate decisions, often turns out to be wrong. Our inability to forecast precisely what's going to happen in the financial sector over the short, medium, and long term reflects the inability of any one person or group—however wise and experienced, and no matter how much theoretical and statistical information may be at one's disposal—to predict the economy's future.

Nor can we discount the fact that any financial system embodies, to varying degrees, what has been called in recent decades by some Christians, including St. John Paul II, as "structures of sin." This is a way of describing the relationship between personal moral error and structures that disorder human relationships and undermine human flourishing. In his 1987 social encyclical *Sollicitudo rei socialis*, John Paul specified that structures of sin "are rooted in personal sin, and thus always linked to the *concrete acts* of individuals who introduce these structures, consolidate them and make them difficult to remove."[22] In an earlier document on sin, John Paul was even more specific about the nature of this connection:

> [S]uch cases of *social sin* are the result of the accumulation and concentration of many *personal sins* . . . of those who are in a position to avoid, eliminate or at least limit certain social evils but who fail to do so out of laziness, fear or the conspiracy of silence, through secret complicity or indifference; of those who take refuge in the supposed impossibility of changing the world, and also those who sidestep the effort and sacrifice required, producing specious reasons of a higher order.[23]

There are thus no "anonymous" actors "out there" or "forces of history" wreaking havoc on peoples' lives. As John Paul wrote, "The real responsibility . . . lies with individuals. A situation—or likewise an institution, a structure, society itself—is not in itself the subject of moral acts. Hence a situation cannot in itself" be sinful or virtuous.[24]

Only persons are moral actors. They are ultimately responsible for the social evil ensuing from the evil acts that proceed from human persons. This need not only take the form of choosing to act in an overtly evil manner. It can also amount to choosing *not* to do good— by being lazy or indifferent. Certainly structures maintained and consolidated by such acts can, as John Paul acknowledged, "influence people's behavior."[25] Yet orthodox Christian ethics firmly holds that in the final analysis people become bad because they freely choose to act wrongly. This insight ought to cause Christians to be careful when they start, for instance, thinking about how to reform financial systems. Policy change certainly matters. Without, however, a commitment on people's part to do good and avoid evil, the effects of policy change are likely to be limited.

Getting Justice Right

No one ideal financial system is immediately derived from either Christian faith or natural reason. That's not just because of sin and its effects. It's also a reflection of a truth that has already been stated but that cannot be repeated enough: while Christianity teaches that one can never choose evil, there are often many ways of doing good that, while differing from one another, don't violate the principles revealed by natural law and divine revelation. There is no uniquely right way to provide, for instance, housing for the homeless. But fraud always constitutes injustice.

Like any sector of the economy, finance is subject to the requirements of justice. And the nature of justice is a topic on which the Christian tradition has long brought very clear principles to bear. A succinct description of these principles may be found in the *Catechism of the Catholic Church*. This text is especially helpful, not least because it draws on a range of sources such as Scripture, the Church Fathers, and natural law to outline these principles, many of which precede the East–West schism of 1054 and Western Christianity's splintering in the Reformation's wake.

Revealingly, the *Catechism*'s discussion of justice follows immediately after its reaffirmation of the classic Christian teaching on common use and private ownership.[26] Beginning with a strong condemnation of theft as a violation of one of the moral absolutes affirmed in the Decalogue,[27] the *Catechism* considers the promises we make to one another in the form of contracts.

Contracts, the *Catechism* specifies, are subject to what Christianity calls commutative justice: that "which regulates the exchanges between persons and between institutions with a strict respect for their rights." Drilling down another level, the *Catechism* immediately adds that commutative justice "obliges strictly." That is strong language. It requires, in the *Catechism*'s words, "safeguarding property rights, paying debts, and fulfilling obligations freely contracted." One reason for this strictness is, as the *Catechism* states, "without commutative justice, no other form of justice is possible."[28] A moment's reflection underlines the truth of this. Life would quickly grind to a halt if everyone considered himself entitled to simply walk away from freely undertaken promises.

Two qualifications need to be made here. First, many parties to a contract may disagree about the meaning of what they have formally decided to adhere to, and what's implied in a given contractual arrangement. Contract law emerged because of the need to resolve such disagreements. Second, commutative justice itself cannot be separated from the demands of other forms of justice. Even if two parties agree to perform certain actions, that doesn't legitimate every single promise made in a given contract. If, for instance, I freely sign a contract that involves me selling myself into slavery, the Christian response would be that the intrinsic immorality and injustice of slavery immediately nullifies the contract.

Understanding the nature of another mode of justice long stressed by Christianity illustrates this point. The *Catechism* defines distributive justice as that "which regulates what the community owes its citizens in proportion to their contribution and needs."[29] The words "contribution" and "needs" are important. They remind us that while distributive justice means ensuring people have what they need, it is also attentive to other criteria such as merit, willingness to assume risk, and how much responsibility a person carries. All other things being equal, this means, for instance, that those who work harder, assume more risk, or take on higher levels of responsibility deserve a higher income or salary than those who decline to do so.

But distributive justice also has implications for the state's role in the economy. It suggests that the state may regulate economic institutions such as contracts and private property—not in an arbitrary way, but rather to ensure that contractual arrangements and the workings of free exchange don't embody significant violations of distributive justice.

The workings of bankruptcy law illustrate the point. Bankruptcy is the process by which an insolvent person or company is declared by the law to be unable to meet his financial obligations. As a result, the bankrupt's property is vested in the courts or some other designated legal trustee who has the responsibility to divide it among the bankrupt's creditors.[30] Bankruptcy law also normally prevents seizure of things that bankrupts require to earn an income[31] or to maintain their families.[32]

Bankruptcy law seeks to reconcile two principles. The first is that, as far as possible, people receive what they are owed in light of the inability of others to pay back all that they owe. The second is that no fulfillment of promises obliges any party to the contract to accept conditions that violate human dignity.[33] From this standpoint, bankruptcy involves consideration of *both* the demands of commutative justice and distributive justice.[34] The creditor's specific claims against the debtors are given attention (commutative justice). At the same time, the claims of all known creditors are pooled by the courts and the debtor's property is treated as if it were the commonly owned property of the creditors (distributive justice).

Here we see the subtle ways in which commutative justice and distributive justice shape each other as we seek to resolve some of life's most thorny economic disputes. Note, however, that the ability of a given society to promote and protect commutative and distributive justice relies on people being willing to accept the decisions of courts, legislatures, and governments. This is what the *Catechism* calls legal justice: that "which concerns what the citizen owes in fairness to the community."[35] It is, after all, the state and the legal system that coordinate these modes of justice. They provide an overall framework that governs the ownership and use of property, and establishes and presides over the arrangements for adjudicating and resolving disputes. Unless people are willing to accept the rulings of courts, human flourishing and the common good become impossible.

But where does the idea of "social justice," which today is endlessly (and not always with great precision) invoked by Christians from all traditions, fit into this picture? The history of the term goes back to the mid-nineteenth century, but it is essentially the same thing as what Aquinas called "legal justice" or "general justice." By "general justice," Aquinas had in mind the virtue of a person's general willingness to promote the *common good* of the communities to which he belongs.

The same common good that is the end of general justice requires more than simply a broad inclination on the part of individuals and groups to promote others' well-being. On one level, as Aquinas specifies, it is a special concern of governments since they have a certain responsibility to promote particular features of the common good. Aquinas notes, however, that it is a concern of *every* citizen: that is, those who participate in some way with the ruling of the community.[36]

The invocation of "social justice" by mid-nineteenth- and early-twentieth-century Christians did not flow from an effort to lend Christian support to every left-of-center economic program. Rather, it represented an attempt to emphasize that everyone has responsibilities to the common good, precisely because legal/general justice had, over the centuries, been reduced to what citizens owed to the state.[37] The point was to broaden people's horizons beyond excessively narrow conceptions of commutative and distributive justice. It means, for instance, that all parties to a contract, such as a creditor and a debtor, must not limit themselves to considering the demands of commutative justice when asking what justice requires. Instead, they must take into account conditions "outside" this particular relationship that affect the human flourishing of the wider community.

That does not imply that Christians are obliged, as a matter of justice, to support every single proposed regulation of the financial sector at the local, national, or international level. As we will see, there are often good reasons to oppose proposed or enacted financial regulations and other forms of intervention. Bailouts, for instance, can often be highly unjust. Attention to the fullness of justice does, however, mean that Christians and others working in the financial sector, whether helping to set monetary policy or managing a hedge fund, need to consider the common good in ways that go beyond, for example, the immediate confines of a contract.

From Theory to Practice

Much more could be said about the Christian conception of justice, but as the example of bankruptcy illustrates, the criteria outlined above have immediate significance for economic life. Far from being the stuff of abstract theorizing, some understanding of factors such as human flourishing, the common good, justice, and the universal destination of material goods is essential if Christians are to be truly concerned with doing good and avoiding evil in the financial sector. After all, Christians cannot act rightly (what some call *orthopraxis*) unless they think correctly (*orthodoxy*): that is, in accordance with the truth about good and evil which Christians believe can be known through the law inscribed on human hearts and divine revelation.

As observed in previous chapters, the language of good, evil, liberty, and the common good and concerns for justice and about poverty permeate the reflections of Scripture, the Church Fathers, medieval theologians, and post-Reformation Christian thinkers on issues of money, usury, time, and the state's role in finance. Now, however, we turn our attention to our own circumstances—societies in which finance occupies a very prominent role in not just everyday economic life but also in shaping the global economy's ups and downs.

Further Reading

Chaput, Charles. "Law and Morality in Public Discourse: How Christians Can Rebuild Our Culture." *Public Discourse*. August 7, 2014. http://www.thepublicdiscourse.com/2014/08/13612.

Gregg, Samuel. "What Is Social Justice?" *Library of Law and Liberty*. April 1, 2013. http://www.libertylawsite.org/liberty-forum/what-is-social-justice.

Grisez, Germain, and Russell Shaw. *Fulfillment in Christ: A Summary of Christian Moral Principles*. Notre Dame, IN: University of Notre Dame Press, 1991.

Hanna, Frank J. *What Your Money Means*. New York: Crossroad Publishing Company, 2008.

Part III

Practice

6

Understanding Capital, Civilizing Capital

There is still a powerful sense around—fair or not—of a whole society paying for the errors and irresponsibility of bankers; of impatience with a return to "business as usual"—represented by still-soaring bonuses and little visible change in banking practices.
Archbishop Rowan Williams, 2011

Criticism and even demonization of those who work in finance are hardly new. The fact that open season was declared (at least rhetorically) on bankers following the 2008 financial crisis should have surprised no one. What was especially revealing was how the criticism didn't just come from those with social democratic inclinations but also from many strong advocates of free markets.

A common complaint across the political spectrum was the apparent absence of accountability on the part of many who worked in the financial industry. Where was the justice, many asked, in the fact that the very same people who had apparently brought the global financial system to the brink of collapse continued to earn very large salaries and bonuses? How could it be that taxpayers, many of whom had been negatively affected by the sharp economic downturn, were left footing the bill for what seemed to be highly imprudent decisions by private capital?

These were entirely reasonable questions. It's also true that hundreds of thousands of people who worked in the world's financial industries lost their jobs from 2007 onward. Entire businesses went out of existence altogether. That's one form of rather brutal accountability—though it didn't always discriminate between those in the financial industry who behaved prudently and those who had been caught up in fueling overheated mortgage markets or selling derivatives whose precise workings couldn't be explained by the people hawking them.

The list of criticisms of private finance by Christians and others is long and detailed. Yet the basic complaints heard from 2008 onward were, with minor variations, essentially the same as criticisms directed at finance for decades. Whether the subject concerned accountability or remuneration, the charges remain remarkably consistent. First and foremost among these is a practice guaranteed to raise many Christians' hackles: speculation.

Speculators and Speculation

The very word "speculation" is a loaded term with deeply negative connotations. In 2004, for instance, a document issued by the World Council of Churches placed money laundering and speculation under the same heading.[1] One does not have to look very far into Christianity's history to find denunciations of financial speculation. In many instances, such commentaries were laced with a heavy dose of anti-Semitism.

Much depends on what is meant by speculation. The *Catechism of the Catholic Church*, for instance, identifies "speculation in which one contrives to manipulate the price of goods artificially in order to gain an advantage to the detriment of others" as "morally illicit."[2] The wording indicates that there *are* legitimate forms of speculation, though these are left unspecified. Writing many decades ago, the Christian social ethicist Oswald von Nell-Breuning, S.J., commented that, with regard to the word *speculation*, "one general definition cannot capture all the nuances."[3] In one of the few contemporary Christian analyses of the subject, Stephen Nakrosis writes, "While it is true that some may use speculative transactions to reap large rewards with little effort, there are also many instances where such trades are a legitimate business tool."[4]

The justice or otherwise of different choices denoted as "speculative" depends on the specifics of a given choice. Gambling, it could be said, is a type of speculation inasmuch as you make a bet based on your guess that you hold a better hand than the house and other participants in the game. Gambling can also involve a choice to put your essential wealth at serious risk and thus endanger the well-being of those who depend on you—in which case gambling is sinful.

Likewise, speculation that relies on telling falsehoods or spreading rumors is wrong because choosing to lie is, in Christian terms, always wrong. It would be equally unjust for a financial firm to try and manipulate the futures market by expressing to others excessive optimism or negativity about the prospects for a given commodity.

All the instances detailed above are very different from the type of speculation that involves making prudential judgments about what one buys and sells on the stock market in light of what one judges is likely to happen in the future on the basis of knowledge, experience, and evidence. Speculation can certainly be abused or used badly. But just as the fact that some banks issue credit to the wrong people doesn't mean that we shut down credit altogether, misuse of speculative techniques does not mean that the practice itself is evil.

At the most basic level, we should bear in mind that an element of speculation is involved with *all* economic activity. *All* of us need to make choices about how we spend and invest our income within a context of perpetual economic change and based on what can only be an imperfect knowledge of the future. Even the mundane activity of placing some of our essential and surplus wealth in a checking account in our local bank involves some speculation insofar as we foresee—as opposed to know with absolute certainty—that (1) the bank will remain solvent, and, if it goes under, (2) something like America's Federal Deposit Insurance Corporation will protect some of our assets.

There are also greater and lesser degrees of speculation, depending on the size of the "bet" and how much one can reasonably forecast the future. When a bank, for instance, grants a two-year small loan to an established business with a track record of on-time loan repayment, it does so with a high degree of certainty that the loan will be repaid.

The scale of the speculation—and the risk—increases in the case of, for instance, a hedge fund that chooses to borrow large amounts of money in order to speculate on the future worth of a given commodity or currency over varying periods of time. "Forward dealings," as they are called, seek to capitalize on expected price movements on goods, products, and shares over a period of time in the hope of selling high and buying low. Such dealings can involve buying or selling products, shares, or commodities at a later date, at a fixed price, in the expectation that, in the meantime, prices will fall (a "bear" transaction) or rise (a "bull" transaction).[5] The higher degree of uncertainty surrounding expected price movements means that the speculative risk is usually higher than a standard small-business loan.

Inevitably, however, Christians must ask if speculation itself is just or unjust. The *first* point to note is that, given the inevitable degree of speculation involved in any economic choice, it is hard to see how speculation per se could be wrong in the sense that every act of adultery, for instance, is intrinsically evil. *Second*, we should recall that many post-Reformation Christian scholars, such as Luis Molina, distinguished speculation (including on money itself) from usury on the basis that the former involved a degree of risk and thus provided a just title to any ensuing profits.

Third, speculation, whether on currencies or commodities, is not a work-free exercise. When a hedge fund decides to go "long" or "short" on the future price of a commodity, it rarely does so on a whim. There is a reason why such firms employ large numbers of forecasters, traders, and even mathematical modelers in an effort to make as accurate a speculative estimate as possible. Though often portrayed as an activity that results in enormous gain on the basis of little labor, speculation often involves quite large amounts of work undertaken by highly knowledgeable groups of people who may lose a great deal (including their jobs) if they make significant errors in judgment.

In the mid-1950s, Johannes Messner listed a number of criteria as essential for helping to determine whether a given act of speculation was just. In addition to insisting that any lying or theft automatically made a speculative act evil, Messner specified that a just act of speculation required (1) a thorough knowledge of the state of the market; (2) adequate study of the influences on the possible development of supply and demand; (3) a serious effort to discern possible tendencies; and (4) a prudent engagement of investments that do not unduly risk the speculator's ability to meet existing business liabilities, despite the factor of uncertainty.[6]

The last of these criteria reflects the requirement to respect the demands of commutative justice. In short, speculation cannot involve unduly undermining your ability to meet your existing contractual obligations to other people and businesses. The first three of Messner's guidelines are essentially counsels to choose and act prudently. They don't prescribe that we "take no risk." Instead they insist that risks be undertaken responsibly.

Implicit to Messner's observations is that those institutions and individuals engaged in speculation ought not to regard other speculators' behavior as the only indication of what constitutes reasonable speculative risk. One would be foolish to ignore market signals before deciding to speculate on anything. There is, however, a type of unthinking herd behavior that follows from blindly following market indicators.[7]

The speed in which transactions occur may magnify the problem. In 2000, the *New York Times* journalist Thomas Friedman famously argued that the Electronic Herd—a conglomeration of the world's investors—"can impose pressures [for good policy] that few governments can resist. It has a self-interest in doing so and it generates in others the self-interest to comply."[8] By the same token, an Electronic Herd of speculators that loses perspective and in which people cease thinking for themselves can do significant and often quite sudden damage.

Given their preexisting obligations to a wider range of people and institutions, financial actors ought to be very careful about simply following the lead of others when engaging in speculation. It helps that, since Messner's time, the financial sector has enhanced its ability to speculate through increasingly sophisticated research and forecasting models. Financial markets do, however, sometimes behave in ways that defy the best forecasting analysis. Nor is any amount of modeling an adequate substitute for basic prudence.

Speculators and the "Real Economy"

Another set of Christian criticisms of speculation concerns its impact on the universal destination of material goods. In this connection, it is quite common to hear the view expressed that speculation diverts capital from being invested in the "real economy."[9]

There is, however, little evidence that investment in various forms of financial speculation somehow reduces the amount of capital available for other ventures. A document published in 1994 by the Pontifical Council for Justice and Peace, for instance, noted that investment in business and corporations in most industrialized countries in the 1980s actually expanded at the very time that investments in financial markets became more widespread.[10]

Other Christians, however, have focused their criticism on the manner in which they believe speculation in particular markets affects the supply of some basic necessities of life. Two popes, Benedict XVI and Francis, have singled out speculation on food prices as especially worrisome.

In 2011, for instance, the former asked, "How can we gloss over the fact that food itself has become an object of speculation or indeed is linked to the development of a financial market which, with no set rules and practically no moral principles, seems attached to the single goal of profit?"[11] Echoing his predecessor, Pope Francis said, "The few derive immense wealth from financial speculation while the many are deeply burdened by the consequences." He also claimed that "speculation on food prices is a scandal which seriously compromises access to food on the part of the poorest members of our human family."[12]

The objection being stated here is that speculators who expect an increase in the price of a commodity and therefore buy many futures contracts effectively drive up the price of goods for which there is presently a high demand. And there are certainly instances in which this type of speculation *can* distort prices. Someone who owns a future position that is larger than the supply of the underlying deliverable commodity available at the competitive price can corner the market and drive up prices. The effect, however, is always transient, and such cases are relatively rare.[13]

More generally, direct evidence for a relationship between price movements and speculative activity is weak. Price increases of the type underscored by the two popes are more adequately explained by dramatic increases in demand for a given good or commodity, combined with a relatively stable supply of that same commodity.[14] Speculators are not responsible for the high or low prices of particular goods over any significant time period. Over the long and medium term the price of food is determined by its degree of scarcity and the forces of supply and demand. If agricultural industries can produce enough food to meet or even exceed demand (through technological innovation and improvements in cultivation), agricultural prices will fall. These are the factors that ultimately determine food prices—not speculation.

Nor is there much evidence to support the argument that the profits made by traders in these instances occur at the expense of the poor. Here we need to understand precisely how speculation works.

If someone needs 2,000 barrels of oil today, he has to pay the present going price of a barrel of oil that's needed today. This is known as the spot price (say, $100). Imagine, however, that you don't need the 2,000 barrels today, but you will need them in one year's time. The futures market allows you to buy these barrels for delivery in one year's time at the futures price of $90. The oil company is willing to sell you these barrels because it guarantees the company a sale. This mutually beneficial arrangement is mediated through a futures contract.

The futures market, however, also allows you to buy barrels of oil without you having any intention of receiving them yourself from the oil company. In these cases, I contract with the oil company for the same 2,000 barrels at the lower futures price with the barrels to be delivered to the holder of the contract in one year's time. By purchasing the contract, I do so in the hope that I can sell it to someone else prior to the delivery at a price closer to the higher spot price.

If the supply of oil remains stable, those who anticipate they will need 2,000 barrels of oil in a year's time will see if I am willing to sell them my contract. In such instances, I break even. If, however, demand for oil grows, they may seek to pay more for my futures contract than they otherwise would. In this instance, I make a profit. But if the oil supply turns out to be greater than expected, then those who need the oil will be able to secure a better deal from someone other than myself. In these circumstances, if I sell my futures contract, it might well be less than the price I paid in the beginning. Hence I lose money.

What's important to note here is that my ability to make a profit as a speculator does not emanate from cheating anyone or from any magical ability on my part to make the price increase and thereby put necessities outside the poor's capacity to pay. Instead, I derive a profit because I correctly estimated that the demand would be greater than the supply at some point in the future. Likewise, my loss would proceed from my failure to ascertain that the supply was going to outstrip demand in a year's time.

Some may dismiss all this as mere gambling. And there may be people who make gamblers' guesses at future supply and demand trends. That's not, however, what most people involved in this type of speculation do. Instead they invest much time and capital in researching production and consumption trends. They also draw on their own and others' knowledge and experience of different industries and markets—including currency markets—before making their choices. In short, labor is involved, as is the willingness to take calculated risks in light of the inevitable degree of uncertainty that marks any economy.

More generally, Christians should also be attentive to the ways in which speculation can contribute to the better use of economic resources for everyone. Speculation—be it in currencies, food, commodities, or anything else—can, for instance, contribute to the relative stability of economic life by helping to calibrate the supply and demand of many goods beyond the short term.

To use the same example of oil: if the futures price for oil goes up, this indicates that a critical mass of those who analyze future trends in the oil industry believe that prices are going to increase in the future. This market signal tells oil producers that they need to find, drill, and extract more oil. But speculation also allows consumers of oil to protect themselves from sudden upward price movements in the future by locking in what they estimate to be a lower future price. And it is not just the producers and consumers who benefit. To the extent that speculation helps to stabilize prices over the medium and long term, it allows everyone to make economic choices in circumstances of greater certainty.

None of this is to deny that problems in speculation can occur. If there is too much liquidity in the financial system, it can result in too much money being used to speculate on a limited number of currencies and commodities. Observe, however, that once again, the problem is *not* speculation per se. It is excessive liquidity in financial markets, often courtesy of excessively loose monetary policy implemented by central banks.

Speculation, Currencies, and Financial Crises

Perhaps the most controversial aspect of speculation concerns speculation on currencies and the way in which some believe speculation can contribute to financial crises. Currency speculation is often seen as an essentially unproductive activity that adds little real value to the economy.

As noted in Chapter 3, early-modern Christian theologians saw no problem in principle with individuals in money markets speculating on the ups and downs of different currencies. By the sixteenth century, some of them had concluded that the value of a currency was determined by supply and demand in the same way that any commodity's value is determined by supply and demand. They also held that people were entitled to make money out of speculating about the future worth of a currency, not least because they determined that this type of risk taking was simply another version of something that Christianity has never found intrinsically problematic: the process of buying something low and selling it high.

Though money markets are more sophisticated today, the substance of currency speculation differs little from the time of Molina and Azpilcueta: it is the buying, selling, and holding of currencies in order to make a profit from favorable fluctuations in exchange rates: that is, the rate at which one currency, such as the Euro, can be exchanged for another, such as the American dollar (otherwise known as a currency pair).

The reasons for exchange-rate fluctuations are not hard to discern. They can change as a result of major upheavals in a country's political setting, or as a consequence of economic developments such as inflation, or of ups and downs in the pace of economic growth. These and many other factors shape the choice of traders to purchase or sell a currency pair. Risk is part and parcel of currency speculation because predicting the effects of some of the changes listed above is very challenging.

In broad terms, currency speculation works in the following way. If a trader takes the view that the American dollar will appreciate in worth against the Japanese yen, then the trader will buy American dollars with Japanese yen. Should the U.S. dollar go up, the investor can buy Japanese yen with the previously purchased U.S. dollars. Their profit is to be found in the arbitrage: that is, the disparity between the currency exchange rates. Likewise, if traders buy American dollars with Japanese yen and the American dollar depreciates, traders stand to lose money because the American dollars aren't worth as much as before.

The primary benefit of such speculation is the way in which it can increase liquidity in the real economy. If, for instance, a German company wants to open a car factory in Britain, it needs to exchange Euros for British pounds. To do so, it needs currency speculators who will buy Euros because they expect this currency to appreciate in value.

The more currency speculators are involved in money markets, the easier it is for traders and investors to buy and sell foreign exchange when they need to do so. That makes international trade much easier. Greater access to foreign currency exchanges also facilitates foreign direct investment by businesses in not just developed economies but also poorer ones. Currency traders and speculators thus effectively function as middlemen. They smooth the process of exchange, making it easier for businesses to access the foreign currencies they need when they need it—all for the cost of a service charge (something explicitly affirmed as a legitimate title by early-modern theologians), and the opportunity to take a risk by speculating on the currency's future worth.

Currency speculation that involves no manipulation, theft, or fraud is thus a legitimate endeavor that often adds value to economic life and helps lubricate its workings across international boundaries. So why then is currency speculation portrayed in such negative terms by some Christians?

The most common criticism is that speculation on a given currency can damage the economic well-being of the country whose currency is being bet against. If, for instance, a country is experiencing economic problems, speculation that its currency is likely to experience a major and sudden decline in value, the argument goes, will exacerbate existing instabilities.

When deciding whether to augment or offload their holdings of that economy's currency, speculators typically look at a range of not always consistent information, such as an economy's competitiveness, labor-market flexibility, inflation rates, and productivity levels (not to mention the choices of larger speculators). If these indicators suggest a country's economy is headed for a fall, speculators will tend to sell their holdings of that country's currency. This increases the supply of that currency in the marketplace and decreases its value. As a broader consensus builds around selling, the currency continues to depreciate, often at an increasing rate. If enough people do this, it is suggested, it is likely to turn speculators' expectations into a self-fulfilling prophecy. And in recessions, wealth creation slows, businesses close and cut back, people lose their jobs, and poverty increases.

That speculators often behave like a herd is undeniable. Sometimes the effects can spill over from one country to others in the region. This happened in the 1997 Asian financial crisis. It's also the case that a speculator who suspends his critical judgment and simply follows the broader speculative pattern because "everyone else is doing it" is, at a minimum, being deeply imprudent.

Nevertheless speculators are *not* ultimately responsible for whether an economy prospers or declines. Currency crises are usually symptoms rather than causes of deeper economic problems. Economies grow (or decay) because of good (or bad) institutional settings and good (or bad) economic policies. In many instances, speculators are often a useful scapegoat for governments unwilling to concede that *their* failure to tackle deep-seated economic problems, such as labor-market inflexibility or the prevalence of widespread corruption in their societies, and *their* mistakes, such as acquiring excessive debt or maintaining excessively low (or high) interest rates, has been the critical enabler of economic decline. A currency crisis was certainly, for instance, part of the financial crisis that engulfed Argentina between 1998 and 2001. But as the financial journalist Paul Blustein writes in his carefully argued analysis of the Argentine meltdown, "Argentina was not a wholly innocent victim—far from it. Democratically elected and appointed Argentine officials made the decisions that led the country down the road to economic disaster."[15]

Nor, we should add, can betting against a currency be viewed as the type of manipulation condemned by, for instance, the *Catechism of the Catholic Church*. Why? Because no manipulation, whether in the form of fraud, lying, theft, or deceit, has occurred. The speculator is simply buying and selling currencies based on his assessment of the economic futures of two or more economies. At no point is he misleading anyone. Nor is he choosing to inflict harm on anyone, let alone an economy.

That said, there *are* forms of speculation that do rely on manipulation and deceit—the type that falls squarely into the category of sinful speculation censured by the *Catechism*. A prominent example was the Libor scandal in 2012.

In simple terms, the Libor (London Interbank Offered Rate) is an average interest rate that's calculated on the basis of major banks in London submitting the interest rates that they presently pay or *expect to pay* (hence, the speculative element) for borrowing from other banks. Libor is used in markets ranging from American derivatives to student loans as a reference point for assessing present *and future* interest rates. It is also a significant factor in many interest-rate swaps and helps to protect floating-rate loans from surges in interest rates.

The Libor scandal involved several banks deflating and inflating the present and estimated future rates they reported, while traders in different banks gave financial enticements to interdealer brokers to disseminate rumors in order to manipulate interest rates.[16] Individual traders did so in order to profit from speculative trades, and to make the financial position of certain banks look better than it was in reality (which became especially important following the 2008 financial meltdown). Equally problematic was the fact that while the practice of misreporting present and expected interest rates was first brought to light in as public a forum as the *Wall Street Journal* in 2008,[17] it took British banks and financial supervisory authorities *four years* to acknowledge and address the problem. Eventually the head of Barclays Bank resigned as a result.[18]

Again, however, the problem was not speculation per se or even Libor itself. The wrongs lay squarely in lying—the spreading of lies with the intent of deceiving others in order to make profits or avoid accountability—and, in some instances, what amounted to bribery. As the *Wall Street Journal* report remarked at the time, "The Libor system depends on banks to tell the *truth* about their borrowing rates. *Fibbing* by banks could mean that millions of borrowers around the world are paying artificially low rates on their loans. That's good for borrowers, but could be very bad for the banks and other financial institutions that lend to them."[19] Failure to adhere to moral absolutes, it turns out, was immensely damaging to the reputation of financial institutions.

Short Term versus Long Term:
A Detached Financial Sector?

Speculation is hardly a new feature of contemporary economic life. Nevertheless, it is often associated in many people's minds with what they believe are two growing and generally undesirable trends within finance. The first is what is often called excessive short-termism in the outlook of private finance. The second is an apparent detachment of those working in financial markets from the deeper realities and complexities of the businesses that make up the real economy. Don't such trends, it might be asked, undermine finance's ability to help realize the universal destination of material goods over the long term? Don't they also promote a type of depersonalization of the economy as a whole?

It is commonly argued that the need of financial firms (especially institutional investors) to generate profits on a quarterly basis to meet their clients' and shareholders' expectations has resulted in financial actors paying less attention to long-term trends and knowing relatively little about the businesses in which they invest capital. As a result, it is claimed, the financial sector's capacity to perform one of its key functions—the management of risk over the medium and long term—has become significantly diminished.

There are negative forms of short-termism in financial markets. If people are incentivized to focus on the short term (such as by the prospect of enhancing one's bonus prospects at year's end), there's a high likelihood they will do precisely that, and in ways that don't always serve stakeholders' interests.

We can't, however, attribute all the problems associated with short-termism to questions of misaligned incentives. Short-termism in financial markets is also reflective of wider societal challenges. These are manifested when, for instance, people take out loans for products and activities they simply can't afford. But the same mindset can be seen in some people's voting habits in democratic systems, or the way that some political leaders seem fixated on the very latest opinion poll when deciding what to do.

When, however, thinking about short-termism and finance, we should recognize that, as Lauzun notes, all the short-term trading in financial markets masks a wider reality: that very little of the enormous amounts of capital being traded in financial markets on a daily basis is actually withdrawn from financial markets. Most capital *stays* in financial markets over the short, medium, and long term. Even many of the short-term trades of this capital serve to provide liquidity for millions of individuals and businesses.[20]

The constant short-term trading in financial markets also helps prices in different markets for the same good or service to gravitate to what is normally the just price, that is, the market price. The potential for what's called *arbitrage* emerges when there is a disparity of prices for the same product in markets. Arbitrage occurs when one can instantaneously buy the same product low in one market and sell it high in another. The fact that the process occurs constantly, very quickly, and at a low level of risk means that it is rarely disruptive. The speed at which financial markets facilitate the process of buying low and selling high in national and international markets helps to establish a convergence of prices for a given good.

While long-term relationships based on reciprocity and growing levels of mutual confidence are important for some of the types of investments that financial markets facilitate, it is also essential that those holding capital can redeploy their assets and resources quickly. Without the ability to do this, the capacity of financial actors to respond quickly to opportunities and problems would be significantly compromised. It's also worth noting that our ability to invest in—or divest from—any particular investment can serve as a strong incentive for those using our capital to do so responsibly.

What then of the claim of growing detachment? Much of the financial sector has, it is sometimes argued, ceased to mediate relationships between creditors, investors, borrowers, and those who deploy the capital. In recent decades, we have witnessed the emergence alongside more traditional banker–client relationships of forms of finance in which few of the participants know each other personally. By their very nature, institutional investors cannot establish the type of close working relationship with businesses that banks often develop with clients. Investing via vehicles such as mutual funds is more anonymous, with investors, borrowers, creditors, and savers treating each other in more abstract ways. It follows, the argument goes, that those managing many modern investment funds or selling financial products have limited interest in anything except their ability to deliver value to those who place their capital in institutional investment vehicles, thereby enhancing their own potential economic well-being.

This narrative contains some truth. The rise of phenomena such as online investing has added a degree of impersonality and abstractness that did not exist before the rise of computerized trading. Yet this story is in need of considerable amendment and even correction.

De Lauzun warns, for instance, that we should be very careful not to mythologize the past in considering this issue. More detached forms of financial interactions didn't simply emerge over the past thirty years. For as long as there have been stock markets, these types of relationships have existed in the financial sector—even, as we have seen, in the late-medieval and early-modern world through devices such as triple contracts.

Nor is there room for false nostalgia. Many of the more traditional forms of bank credit and investment that we often associate with pre-1970s finance—before it underwent significant deregulation—were not and are not always the most suitable forms of intermediaries.[21] Some loans, for instance, *are* complicated because they involve multiple partners and multiple transactions. Many contemporary forms of finance, while often complicated and depersonalized, are focused on pooling capital and risk from multiple partners in order to put financial muscle behind ideas, products, and industries on a scale that smaller financial actors and many more traditional forms of bank credit could not and cannot support, not least because of their lower risk threshold.

The traditional forms of finance, one might argue, would have also struggled to incorporate the millions of new investors in stock markets and other forms of finance. Thanks to new technologies and sophisticated financial products designed to meet the varying needs, risk thresholds, and responsibilities of millions of people, more people are now involved and have a direct stake in financial markets than at any other time of history. This in itself is surely a good thing, inasmuch as the ability to participate in capital and stock markets and enjoy their benefits was once confined to already-wealthy segments of the population. The cost may be more depersonalized relationships. Yet without these new forms of investment, it is hard to imagine how modern finance could have been put to work for so many people.

The Knowledge Issue

The detachment issue, however, involves more than the varying forms in which capital is mobilized and put to work. As anyone who works on Wall Street or in the City of London can attest, traders buy and sell shares every day in publicly traded corporations about which they know relatively little. How, one might ask, is it possible for traders to really know anything substantial about the many publicly traded companies whose shares pass (electronically) through their hands hundreds of time on any given trading day?

One response is to point out that part of the underlying rationale for markets in general is that market prices are an imperfect but relatively accurate way to aggregate a great deal of dispersed information about the fundamental economic health of a range of assets. Changes in market prices thus normally reflect the aggregate knowledge of what people in the marketplace think is happening to thousands of assets and companies and what's likely to happen to these investments and businesses in the future.

So while it is true that a trader may know little about the intimate details of what is happening in any number of businesses, the market price of shares in that company *does* tell the trader something about the relative health of companies compared to the myriad number of other possible companies in which one can invest. There is no other way to attain this type of information in a market of millions of investors and businesses.

One factor that may account for the sense that financial markets have become detached from the rest of the economy is the reliance of many financial actors on mathematical models and computer modeling. The human element, we are told, is steadily diminished through the inevitable instrumentalization and objectification of companies and capital that are encouraged by the use of such tools.

Yet the issue here is surely less about detachment and more about people in the financial sector placing excessive faith in the capacity of mathematics to model economic realities. A major warning signal should have been the failure and bailout of the Wall Street firm Long-Term Capital Management after it lost $4.6 billion in the wake of the 1997 Asian financial crisis and the debt meltdown that struck Russia in 1998.[22] LTCM had deployed extensive economic modeling on derivatives to make significant profits, only to find that the models turned out to be not so accurate in their predictive ability.

LTCM's collapse demonstrated the folly of financial firms and strategies excessively relying on what the economic historian Niall Ferguson calls the "scientific pretensions" of much contemporary economics. We should certainly welcome the opportunities that such methods have provided us in terms of managing risk, just as much as we welcome the ways that mathematical modeling has improved the efficiency of many other parts of our lives, ranging from air travel to weather forecasting. Yet in finance, we are dealing with probabilities of risk—not least because of the human element—and even the best mathematical model can only narrow the range of risk to a certain extent in light of uncertainty.[23] And this is acceptable—as long as the limits of this approach remain understood. The problem isn't the tool itself but a hubristic confidence in mathematics and forecasting models on the part of those using it.

A similar point was underscored by Benedict XVI in a letter written in 2009 on the eve of the G20 Summit in London to then-British Prime Minister Gordon Brown. The pope underscored that financial instruments and strategies are human creations that, if they become objects of blind faith for those working in financial markets, can sow the seeds of financial meltdowns.[24] Financial markets consist, after all, of imperfect people, and therefore of imperfect human institutions that reflect and can magnify such flaws.

Earlier that year, Pope Benedict had suggested that the financial sector's fragility owed much to the ever-increasing short-term buying and selling of financial instruments for their own sake alongside widespread preoccupation with the technicalities of creating and manipulating new financial vehicles. This had, the pope added, distracted much of the financial sector from one of its primary roles of helping to bridge the present and the future.[25] Put another way, finance had turned inward to focus on itself.

In these words, Benedict hit upon a home truth. One of the genuine problems characterizing financial markets in the lead-up to 2008 was how many in the financial world became increasingly fixated with developing ever-more-complicated risk instruments in which the complication itself became seen as enhancing the value of the product—to the extent, one might add, that those selling such products didn't even understand the products themselves.

If someone selling a product, financial or otherwise, has no real grasp of how that financial product works (let alone a genuine understanding of the real level of risk associated with the product), then justice toward real and potential customers requires that he make an effort to understand the product. If he still fails to understand the product or even starts to see fundamental flaws, he should refrain from selling it.

This is simply a case of putting ourselves in our neighbor's position. What would we think of someone else's choice to sell me a debt instrument in which there is no real way to quantify the risk? Again, it is not the financial instrument itself that is at fault. What is at fault are the humans who create such products, who don't fully understand them, and who sell them to people without acknowledging that they don't understand the product themselves.

Just and Unjust Compensation

This brings us to a subject concerning the financial sector that arouses the wrath of even many committed Christians who affirm the moral and economic case for free markets—the issue of compensation. How, many wonder, could it have been that those working in the finance sector in, for instance, 2007 and 2008 were earning such large bonuses? Given the scale of the subsequent crisis and the extent of bad judgments on the part of so many people in finance, de Lauzun is surely correct to say that compensation levels in the lead-up to the 2008 crisis were "aberrant."[26] In many respects, it reflected a misalignment between compensation, quality of performance, and a lack of accountability. Following the financial crisis of 2008, there was no shortage of politicians from left, center, and right who proposed, perhaps with a view to humoring angry voters, to use legislation to address what many regard as a substantial problem.

In his analysis of compensation in the financial sector, the economist, banker, former chief policy advisor to Margaret Thatcher, and Evangelical Anglican Christian Brian Griffiths sums up the objections to compensation levels for those working in finance as the following: (1) bonuses encourage bankers to focus on the short term instead of the long term; (2) the compensation offered is absurdly beyond what is merited; (3) the size of the bonuses paid out to employees by banks bailed out by taxpayers is unjust; and (4) compensation does not reflect a solid alignment of the interests of employees and owners.[27]

On the other side of the ledger, Griffiths observes that compensation levels in the financial industry do reflect the workings of a free labor market—and the moral significance of free movements of labor is closely associated with freedom of association, something that Christian social ethics has always upheld as important for human flourishing. When faced with a highly competitive labor market (such as the financial sector), Griffiths adds, high compensation is one way of retaining talented and hard-working employees in a business that demands incredibly high effort and long hours—something that is reflected in a high rate of turnover. And not all that turnover is voluntary. People deemed to be inadequate performers are regularly let go.

Given this context, how might financial firms think through this issue in a principled manner? A Christian might point to the requirements of commutative and distributive justice. One requirement of commutative justice is equality in exchange. In the case of remuneration, this means that salaries and bonuses must match the service provided.

A concern for commutative justice means that financial firms should regularly ask themselves whether such a trader's compensation corresponds with the value he provides to his clients and the firm that employs him. A great basketball player may attract many people to watch the sport, which helps the basketball industry pay for the salaries and infrastructure that allows millions to watch games they would otherwise be unable to see. So, too, a trader who increases the value of the assets of his clients is able to establish a correspondence between his compensation and what he delivers to his clients and employers. To this extent, the requirements of commutative justice are met, at least in principle. If, conversely, the value of assets under the trader's supervision declines, then (all other things being equal) commutative justice suggests a corresponding reduction in salary and bonuses. In many firms, this actually happens.

Looking at the same issue through the lens of distributive justice, a firm can ask itself what employees are reasonably owed in light of what everyone else in a financial firm is reasonably owed. The precise way in which these requirements are cashed out can vary. Much depends on the nature of the firm itself, the position someone occupies in that firm, and what he merits in light of what everyone else in that company merits. It's reasonable, for instance, for those who assume very senior executive positions in a business to be paid a great deal more than first-year employees. There is no hard and fast rule, however, that can be universally applied to make such determinations.

What then can a Christian say about the compensation for those working in the financial sector in general vis-à-vis the rest of society? Part of the assessment from the standpoint of distributive justice involves considering whether the earnings of those in the financial sector are commensurate to their contribution to the economy and the common good. If, for instance, the financial sector of a country is relatively small and doesn't constitute a large segment of the economy, it's reasonable to assume that the compensation might not be as large as, for instance, another country in which the financial sector is the single biggest contributor to the overall growth of wealth.

Rewards, Justice, and Equality

The compensation question and its implications for the wider economy raise the issue of whether compensation levels in finance reflect a broader problem of injustice. This is not inconceivable. As Philip Booth writes, "[I]f the financial system has developed so that it allows some to profit *at the expense of* others or so that it excludes most people from its benefits then the common good might not be fulfilled also."[28] That would be evidence of a serious market failure requiring some form of remedy. It might also point to even more worrisome problems in the financial sector, such as widespread fraud and systematic corruption.

At the same time, it isn't immediately obvious from a Christian perspective that people earning high compensation in the financial sector (or any segment of the economy for that matter) compared to what's earned by those in other sectors in the economy usually constitutes distributive injustice. Significant income gaps between those working in finance and everyone else don't necessarily mean that "everyone else" is losing out or that significant violations of distributive justice are occurring. Nor is there anything in the Christian tradition to suggest that realizing egalitarianism in the sense of a gradual leveling of everyone's income across the economy to the more or less same level (let alone levels predetermined by the state) is a required or desirable social and economic end—let alone a demand of social justice. Instead the stress is on accountability for what one has and does as well as acting justly toward others. Scripture doesn't criticize the wealthy because they are richer than others. They are criticized, often fiercely, when they engage in fraud, when they forget their real and direct responsibilities to the poor, or when their wealth becomes their god.

Attention to some of the criteria of distributive justice also brings more clarity to thinking about compensation issues in finance vis-à-vis other segments of the economy. In the first place, many people in finance share in the *risk* undertaken by the investment firms in which they work. Readiness to assume risk has long been recognized as a ground for earning more than those who decide not to take the same risk. Most civil servants, for instance, are paid less than someone in finance, at least partly because civil servants generally enjoy far more job security than people working in the financial sector.

Second, many of those who work in financial markets today take on significant *responsibilities* for the common good that, at least indirectly, go beyond the vital task of wealth creation. They are effectively entrusted, for instance, by the rest of us with the not-so-simple task of ensuring that liquidity is more or less permanently available to the wider economy. Without people with the skills, experience, and work habits necessary to perform this task, economic life would be generally less creative and less productive. That would undermine everyone's economic well-being. The same people also manage and invest the capital of millions of people—not just the super-rich but also those with modest retirement accounts or who place some spare capital into a variety of investment funds. In short, they have effectively been entrusted with the financial futures and retirements of vast numbers of families and individuals. That is no small undertaking.

Third, the financial sector undertakes a vital function in modern capitalist economies that isn't always appreciated by others: the formation of prices for capital in usually imperfect market-competitive conditions. Those employed in financial markets invest considerable time and energy in spotting misallocations of capital and helping to correct misalignments in ways that promote profit and minimize losses. They also have to make difficult decisions about what are healthy and unhealthy investment possibilities based partly on research but also on imperfect information about future possible opportunities and liabilities. To this extent, they play a significant role in promoting a better and more efficient allocation of resources throughout the entire economy. This helps investors make better decisions about how much to invest and aids those looking for capital to make less risky, more informed choices concerning how much to borrow and for how long. More generally, better and more accurate pricing of capital and resources helps everyone—wealthy, middle-class, and the less well-off—to make choices about how to use the essential and surplus capital at their disposal in light of their needs, wants, and responsibilities.

These factors don't justify every single remuneration arrangement in the financial industry. Those who are paid high compensation despite consistently poor performance or who make very serious mistakes about how they invest other people's capital obviously don't merit their pay.

One approach often suggested (especially in the aftermath of financial meltdowns) for addressing these and other problems is for governments to place caps on compensation. This, it is held, seems to be the only way to prevent compensation in the financial sector from reaching absurd levels. Another suggestion has been to introduce special taxes specifically targeted at not just the corporate profits of financial firms but also their employees' salaries and bonuses.

Yet, as Griffiths notes, efforts to cap compensation in one sector of finance will very likely result in people leaving to go to other sections of the financial industry or simply starting their own businesses. We also know that attempts to control financial sector compensation from the top down, whether through caps or by levying special taxes, have failed.[29] In any event, it's simply impossible for governments or regulators to know enough about the different performance levels of thousands of individuals in hundreds of banks and investment firms to make all-embracing assessments of what constitutes just compensation.

A more productive approach that might address compensation questions—and which financial firms themselves have a long-term interest in addressing—would be to require high-level traders and the directors of financial firms to have some of their own skin in the game. In their analysis of the 2001 Enron scandal, David Campbell and Stephen Griffiths point out: "One has to stretch the point to say that the executives of large public companies are exposed to the economic risks of failure in any significant way, and certainly they are more or less completely cocooned from the most fundamental market pressure, fear of personal bankruptcy."[30] Speaking of joint stock companies in the eighteenth century, Adam Smith identified the core of the problem: "The directors of such companies . . . being the managers of other people's money than their own, it cannot be well-expected that they should watch over with the same vigilance. . . . Negligence and profusion must always prevail, more or less, in the management of such a company."[31]

There would be a significant trade-off associated with requiring those working in finance to have more personally at stake. Without limited liability, some very talented and good people will simply decline to go into those forms of commerce where limited liability doesn't apply. Yet it is worth considering how director and employee compensation could reflect a greater assumption of the risks of the activity. De Lauzun notes that this was once the rule for the partners of many Wall Street firms. That doesn't mean that such requirements should be legislated. But if firms were to re-embrace this principle, it would be more than simply good public relations. In many cases, it would help to establish firmer links between compensation arrangements and performance.

Finance, Regulation, and the State

Proposals for more just compensation arrangements should be distinguished from issues of equality. It may well be that compensation levels in the financial sector contribute to growing economic inequality, and growing economic inequality may well be criticized on other grounds. As mentioned, however, the immediate question is whether those who work in the financial industry are doing well at the direct expense of others. The more general question of economic inequality requires a broader approach that goes beyond a particular industry's specifics if it is to be addressed in a just and comprehensive manner.

That said, nothing in the preceding analysis rules out taxation of the corporate profits of financial firms (or another other business) or the earnings of those working in finance (or any other industry that pays very high compensation) in order to help realize the universal destination of material goods. Christians can and do argue about the extent, prudence, and justice of different forms of taxation. But Christian ethics has never viewed taxation per se as theft.

Nor do reason and Christian faith preclude direct or indirect regulation of the financial sector. Christian social ethics disputes the notion that the economy can exist in a legal or regulatory void. At the same time, Christian ethics is opposed to regulatory regimes that either by design or in practice nullify economic freedom. Between these polarities of no regulation and endless regulation, however, there is considerable room for Christians to debate among themselves and with non-Christians the scope, character, and fairness of varying forms of economic regulation and other forms of government intervention.

Before 2008, the world's financial markets were subject to literally thousands of regulations. They also operated in an environment in which there was no shortage of regulatory authorities. Nevertheless, following the Great Recession, governments across the globe faced calls for greater regulation of the financial sector. And throughout North America and much of Western Europe, new financial regulations were introduced. The Dodd–Frank Wall Street Reform and Consumer Protection Act (2010), for instance, represented the most significant change to the regulatory framework governing the financial sector in the United States since the New Deal. This was preceded by governments and central banks bailing out, and in some cases taking over, several private financial actors.

In retrospect it is hard to deny that governments and regulators contributed in their own way to the financial meltdown.[32] Griffiths and others have pointed to the responsibility of those politicians who legislated to cajole banks into making sub-prime mortgage loans, central bankers who kept interest rates too low for too long, ratings agencies who assigned high ratings to many securities that turned out to be built on mortgage-based derivatives, regulators who failed to recognize the growth of dangerously high leverage levels in the system, as well as ordinary citizens who happily borrowed when they really couldn't afford to.[33]

Though not opposed in principle to government institutions regulating finance, Christians writing about such matters in the past also believed there were limits to such action. Nor were they afraid to underline the possible economic dysfunctionalities and injustices that could flow from particular types of intervention. And while the state's involvement in finance has become more extensive and complex in our own time, there remains much that Christianity can contribute to ongoing debates on this subject.

Further Reading

Blustein, Paul. *And the Money Kept Rolling In (and Out): Wall Street, the IMF, and the Bankrupting of Argentina*. New York: Public Affairs, 2005.

Booth, Philip. "Catholic Social Teaching and the Financial Crash." In Philip Booth (ed.), *Catholic Social Teaching and the Market Economy*. London: IEA, 2014.

Lowenstein, Roger. *When Genius Failed: The Rise and Fall of Long-Term Capital Management*. New York: Random House, 2000.

Schlag, Martin, and Juan Andrés Mercado (eds.). *Free Markets and the Culture of the Common Good*. London: Springer, 2012.

7

The Common Good, the State, and Public Finance

Many enhance kingly power beyond reasonable and just lim-
its—some to gain the prince's favor and to amass private wealth.
The most pestilent of men are not concerned with honesty and are
commonly found in the courts of princes. Others reason to the con-
viction that an increase in royal majesty enhances the protection
of public welfare. But they are mistaken. As in the case of other
virtues, power has definite limits, and when it goes beyond limits,
power does not become stronger but rather becomes completely
debilitated and breaks down.

Juan de Mariana, S.J.[1]

From the beginning of the Christian church, it's view of government has not been negative. Despite the often-brutal persecution of Christians by the Roman authorities, nowhere does one find in Scripture or the Church Fathers any claim that government is an essentially illegitimate institution, let alone the suggestion that any form of state coercion whatsoever is wrong.

Alongside this basic affirmation, Christianity has always insisted there are boundaries to the state's authority—including over the economy—not the least being that political institutions are as subject to the demands of justice as the choices and actions of individuals, families, and other communities. Saint Augustine put it well when he wrote in his *City of God*: *Remota itaque iustitia quid sunt regna nisi magna latrocinia* ("Justice being taken away, then, what are kingdoms but great robberies?").[2]

As Chapter 4 demonstrates, there's little doubt that Christian theologians in the past believed that state institutions had concrete responsibilities regarding the establishment and maintenance of monetary and fiscal order. The same thinkers, however, were not afraid to underline the limits of state power in this area or to criticize imprudent or unjust decisions by government officials that affected the financial system.

Though very few Christians today argue for either regulation-free financial systems or a complete state monopoly of finance, it was hardly surprising that many Christians argued for greater regulation in the wake of the financial crisis in 2008. This ranged from calls to prohibit particular forms of speculation to establishing formal minimal capital requirements and even the establishment of a world central bank. Other Christians (including myself) expressed reservations about whether many of these proposals would be efficacious in achieving their goals, and in some cases, might make bad situations worse, or could even violate particular principles of justice.

These legitimate debates among Christians will no doubt continue, not least because there is no uniquely correct Christian view of the state's positive policy responsibilities in this area. There is nothing in Christian social ethics to suggest, for instance, that the state must enjoy a monopoly of the money supply; nor, however, does Christianity prohibit governments from establishing such a monopoly.

There is no shortage of subjects that could be considered in any reflection on the state's role vis-à-vis finance. Some, however, are more important than others. There are also some issues into which Christianity has more direct insight. Prominent among these is the issue of *moral hazard* and the extent to which particular governmental policies can encourage irresponsible behavior by private financial actors.

Hazardous Lending, Evading Responsibility

The origins of the term "moral hazard" lie in neither economics nor theology. They have been traced back to the seventeenth century and the development of the insurance industry.[3] Today it describes a phenomenon summarized by Nobel economist Paul Krugman as "any situation in which one person makes the decision about how much risk to take, while someone else bears the cost if things go badly."[4]

When economists use the term, they don't typically mean immoral or fraudulent behavior. Rather, it is about circumstances, policies, and institutions that encourage individuals and businesses to take on excessive risk, most notably with assets and capital entrusted to them by others, because they safely assume they will not pick up the bill for any failure. Hence, while profits remain private, losses are socialized. Heads, I win. Tails, taxpayers lose. The higher the extent of the guarantee, the greater is the risk of moral hazard.

A good example of how this occurs through government institutions may be seen in central banks. They assume the role of providing liquidity—either directly and/or through organizing private banks, or open-market operations—when a banking system has apparently run out of liquidity. A defining characteristic of a central bank is that lenders of last resort cannot go bankrupt.

The difficulty is that the very existence of a lender of last resort can encourage private financial actors to imagine that they are "too big to fail." Indeed, if they possess enough systematic presence in a given financial system, they have reason to assume they will be provided with liquidity by a central bank if a failed endeavor threatens their solvency, no matter how foolish or irresponsible their behavior. As a result, such financial actors will become complacent and take risks that become increasingly irresponsible over time.

Economists and others have long debated the overall significance of moral hazard, the extent to which it is a real problem, and the ways it might be minimized. In a *Financial Times* column in 2007, for instance, a prominent member of the Clinton and Obama administrations' economic teams, Larry Summers, argued that we should beware of what he called "moral hazard fundamentalism." This was, he said, "as dangerous as moral hazard itself." By this, Summers meant that ruling out significant government economic intervention on the grounds that it might encourage moral hazard would itself be irresponsible.

That same year, however, another Nobel economist, Vernon Smith, warned that the activities of the mortgage lenders Fannie Mae and Freddie Mac were underpinned by the assumption that, as government-sponsored enterprises with lower capital requirements than private institutions, they could always look to the federal government for assistance if an unusually high number of their clients defaulted. Both Fannie Mae and Freddie Mac, Smith noted, were always understood as "implicitly taxpayer-backed agencies."[5] And so it was that they continued what are now recognized as their politically driven and fiscally irresponsible lending policies until both suffered the ignominy of being placed in federal conservatorship in September 2008.

It is curious, however, that despite the word "moral" being part of the description, Christian reflection on finance has said very little about moral hazard. An analysis in 1994 of the financial sector's effects upon the rest of the economy commissioned by the Pontifical Council for Justice and Peace, for instance, did not discuss moral hazard and how it can incentivize financial institutions to behave irresponsibly.[6] Nor, on the other hand, does the economics literature on moral hazard contain much reflection on why the adjective "moral" is attached to the word "hazard." If there is no moral dimension, why are these situations not simply described as instances of "risk hazard"?

It may be that the word "moral" reflects some innate, albeit largely unexpressed, awareness that there is something ethically questionable about creating situations in which people are severely tempted to make imprudent choices. To employ an analogy from Christian moral theology, the one who creates what is called "an occasion of sin" bears some indirect responsibility for the choices of the person tempted by this situation to do something imprudent or just plain wrong.

Given the truth of human fallibility, almost everyone will take excessive risks at different points in their lives. For some people, it will be with their business. Others will behave in an excessively risky manner with their own and others' financial resources. As a consequence, some people will suffer losses.

In such circumstances, individual Christians and communities should be ready to help those in genuine need. That's a requirement of mercy and justice. Yet Christians also can and should ask questions concerning the extent to which people have been encouraged to engage in irresponsible behavior by particular policies.

At the same time, the phenomenon of moral hazard doesn't excuse individual and institutional financial actors from their irresponsible actions. Certainly one can be incentivized to act in a particular way, and one of the key insights of economics is that incentives matter. Christians, however, don't believe that humans are automatons that simply react to stimuli. That means people *can* choose to take reasonable rather than imprudent risks. Hence they are accountable for their actions. To deny accountability or to dismiss it in the name of people being subject to wider forces outside their control would not do justice to the Christian belief that humans are free and therefore accountable for their choices.

To Bail or Not to Bail

The moral-hazard dilemma pressed itself heavily on the consciousness of many Americans and Western Europeans from 2008 onward, when governments were confronted with decisions about whether to rescue several huge financial institutions. The uncertainty about what to do at such times is evident from the accounts authored by some of the significant policymakers involved in the often chaotic decision-making process.[7]

On one level, many were wary of the potential knock-on effects of allowing financial institutions of a certain size to fail because of the financial sector's interconnectedness: something that goes beyond national boundaries. But many of the same citizens and legislators were reluctant to bail out financial institutions that had behaved irresponsibly. This, it was held, would send a signal to the rest of the financial industry: that is, if you are big enough we will not let you fail.

On the other side of the bailout equation, there is some evidence that many bankers did indeed see taxpayers as those who would save them from insolvency. In September 2008, for example, the Anglo Irish Bank was facing the prospect of a meltdown in the wake of a collapse in Ireland's housing market bubble. In a recorded phone call, two senior executives, John Bowie and Peter Fitzgerald, discussed what the bank should do. Bowie noted that he and his colleagues had asked for a 7 billion euro bailout from the Irish regulator. The bailout was presented to the regulator as a bridge between Anglo Irish's present insolvency and a period in the future when the bank would presumably be solvent. To this, Fitzgerald responded by saying, "so it is bridged until we can pay you back . . . which is never." After these words, the two men laughed.

A few minutes later in their discussion, Bowie told Fitzgerald that Anglo Irish required in fact much more than 7 billion euros. He had, however, used that figure because he wanted to entice regulators into a series of future bailouts: "The strategy here is you pull them in, you get them to write a big [check] and they have to keep, they have to support their money." To this Bowie added, "If they saw . . . the enormity of it up front, they might decide . . . they have a choice. . . . They might say the cost to the taxpayer is too high. But . . . if it doesn't look too big at the outset, if it looks big, big enough to be important, but not too big that it kind of spoils everything."[8]

The bankers concerned later stated that they had no intention of misleading the Irish Central Bank, though conceded that their language had been inappropriate and imprudent.[9] However one interprets their words, the economist Roger Koppl is surely right to say, "This conversation suggests that the 'moral hazard' problem created by 'too big to fail' is quite real and something that directly and self-consciously influences the thinking of financial institutions."[10]

There is other evidence to suggest that signals of a willingness to bail out do weaken fiscal responsibility and encourage imprudent risk taking on the part of comparably sized financial firms. One study found, for instance, that "the rescue of Bear Stearns [in March 2008] caused a significant reduction in market discipline."[11] Saving Bear Stearns, it seems, *did* facilitate a moral hazard problem. The same analysis also suggested, however, that "[d]espite the failure of Lehman Brothers, market discipline declined further after September 2008."[12] On this basis, the authors conclude that those in charge should "stick to a strict 'always-or-never' bail-out policy in order to minimize fiscal and social losses."[13] This need for a consistency of position was underscored in 2009 by the monetary policy historian Anna Schwartz while reflecting on the Federal Reserve's actions in 2008:

> [T]he trouble with the way the Fed operated when it rescued Bear Stearns [was that] the market then believed this was a signal of the way the Federal Reserve would perform. If the Fed and the Treasury made a candid statement to the market: We will help a bank, which basically is solvent. We will not do that for a bank, which is on the verge of bankruptcy. And then the market understands there are principles. That's why when Lehman Brothers was permitted to fail, the market was simply bewildered. Because here you had treated Bear Stearns in this kindly fashion, and what reason was there not to do the same when Lehman Brothers arose?[14]

Again, there's no uniquely correct approach to this dilemma from the standpoint of Christian concern for justice. The same framework, however, does indicate the need for some degree of accountability on the part of those who choose to behave irresponsibility. From this perspective, it is surely preferable to put failed financial institutions—including large ones—through managed bankruptcy procedures that embody principles of commutative and distributive justice. In that way, some degree of responsibility can be established. Second, an effort should be made to minimize as far as possible the structures and incentives that might encourage individuals and institutional investors to take excessive risk. Insurance should be precisely that: insurance against potential catastrophe rather than a device that allows one to keep profits while passing on the costs of failure to others.

At the same time, Christian ethics would suggest that central banks should be ready to act when there is a genuine sense that the financial system as a whole—rather than simply a few politically well-connected but also bankrupt institutions—is in genuine danger, and no other institution is capable of responding to the situation. That would be in accordance with what's called the principle of subsidiarity (well articulated in modern Catholic social teaching but whose formulation owes much to the early-seventeenth-century Calvinist theologian Johannes Althusius), according to which "higher" institutions (such as the state) should directly intervene only when it is manifestly obvious that "lower" communities are incapable of addressing a problem, and then only on a temporary basis.

It may well be that the systematic stability of the financial system and therefore the common good is threatened by a particular bank failure. Here a bailout might well be legitimate—provided those paying for the bailing out are compensated for their loss, and that those responsible for the bank's failure are held accountable for their mistakes and errors. There is something fundamentally wrong with allowing people in finance to be capitalists in good times and socialists in bad times.

There is, however, another factor that should be considered when thinking through the ethics and economics of bailouts. The low regard in which many today hold the financial industry surely owes something to the perception that the financial industry, despite its contributions to wider economic meltdowns, benefits from assistance that is not accorded to other segments of the economy. To intervene in order to save the financial system is one thing. It is quite another to intervene because a bank in trouble happens to enjoy good political connections. The latter may well amount to what's often called "crony capitalism."

Crony capitalism is not criminal activity or outright corruption—though it verges on, and often enters, these spheres. Crony capitalism involves people's ability to harness government power to stack the economic deck in their favor instead of creating, refining, and offering products and services at competitive prices. While the market's outward form is maintained, its essential workings are supplanted by the struggle to ensure that governments, legislators, and regulators favor you at other people's expense. In that sense crony capitalism certainly constitutes a form of redistribution, but one that is highly unjust: away from taxpayers, consumers, and businesses focused on creating wealth, and toward the more organized, powerful, and politically connected.

In this context, one need not be a conspiracy theorist to worry about the revolving door that exists between some sectors of the financial industry and senior positions in central banks and government finance departments.[15] It's hardly surprising that people with significant private-sector financial expertise will be recruited for public service in the world's treasuries or central banks. Nor should we simply assume impropriety. That would be unfair. As noted at the beginning of this book, the overwhelming majority of banks that fail in America are *not* bailed out. Nevertheless, Christians should be attentive to, and critical of, the injustice that occurs when a bank or investment firm is bailed out primarily because of its good political connections rather than a genuine concern for the common good.

Regulation and Its Limits

Bailouts are an instance of government regulation, albeit of the dramatic type. After 2008, it become commonplace to hold that one reason for the financial meltdown was deregulation of the financial sector from the 1980s onward, whether it took the form of simplifying the rules that govern economic life or a reduction in the overall number of regulations.

Such arguments are often prevalent in Christian circles. In 2009, for instance, Archbishop Rowan Williams claimed, "It is a little too easy to blame the present situation on an accumulation of individual greed, exemplified by bankers or brokers, and to lose sight of the fact that governments committed to deregulation and to the encouragement of speculation and high personal borrowing were elected repeatedly in Britain and the United States for a crucial couple of decades."[16]

From a Christian standpoint, regulation in itself is not problematic. The device of contract, for instance, that is central to commutative justice acquires much of its force from the participants' assumption that there are courts to mediate contractual disputes and that the rulings of courts (who themselves are bound by precedent and legislation) are binding. Nor is there any Christian objection in principle to governments having a role in, for instance, defining and enforcing safeguards for consumers and investors. Rather, the disputes among Christians concerning regulation invariably concern the extent and type as well as the prudence of doing so in different conditions.

It often seems the case that some Christians are inattentive to the ways in which various forms of regulation can help facilitate excessive risk taking and imprudent behavior. Take for instance international and domestic regulations that require banks to maintain reserve capital (or what's often called regulatory capital)—defined as the bank's assets minus its liabilities.[17]

The purpose of maintaining reserves is to protect the bank (and its shareholders) from the effects of bad investments or general market turndowns. A bank may have $1 billion in assets and $800 million in liabilities. Such a bank can weather a 20 percent drop in the value of its assets and still remain solvent. If, however, the same bank experiences a 30 percent drop in its asset value, it cannot pay all its debts and is thus technically insolvent.

By imposing capital requirements on banks, its proponents maintain, governments can insulate themselves and taxpayers from finding themselves completely on the hook in the case of a bank failure. Of course, not all loans and investments are equally risky. Reserve capital requirements therefore associate different levels of capital requirements with the different risk levels attached to different forms of investments.

There are, however, a number of problems associated with such policies. Regulators, for instance, simply don't have—and never will have—the ability to specify a unique capital requirement for every single investment or loan. This becomes even more improbable given the complexity of any number of financial instruments. Hence, assigning a capital requirement is always a "guesstimate," as the risk associated with any investment or loan cannot be determined in advance and is constantly changing.

A further complication emerges as a result of banks and financial houses seeking to maximize return by engaging in what's called regulatory arbitrage: they want to hold as few assets as possible in order to increase the amount they have invested and on which they hope to make a profit. Thus they engage in practices like securitization. This is the consolidation of a series of different debts—such as credit-card debt, mortgage debt, and commercial debt—in the form of a security, followed by the sale of that security to individual and institutional investors. If the bank can obtain a risk rating on the security because it is determined that the low-risk assets outweigh those assets with high-risk rating, then the capital reserve requirement for a given segment of the security (called a tranche) is less than it might have otherwise been as a stand-alone product.

The upside of regulatory arbitrage is that it stands to produce greater returns for the bank and investors. Moreover, managing and leveraging risk is central to what private finance does. The downside is that reasonably assessing the risk associated with these types of products is very hard.

The point, however, is that this type of arbitrage is driven in part by regulations ostensibly designed to stabilize and reduce the amount of risk in financial markets. The very nature of regulatory arbitrage is such that each new regulation is an opportunity for arbitrage. A typical response of financial institutions to increased regulation is to hire very creative people to find ways "to arbitrage" the new regulatory arrangements. Regulators may react by closing a loophole. But the same smart people will then work out how to arbitrage the changed situation.

The fact of regulatory arbitrage is not a reason to decline to regulate the financial industry. The potential for such arbitrage should not, however, be ignored by Christians whenever new regulations are proposed.

Another side effect associated with financial regulation is the way in which it can contribute to people making seriously wrong choices. This can be illustrated by the example of something of which many Christians have been very critical: payday loans.

Payday loans are small, short-term unsecured loans that rely not on the debtor providing the creditor with some asset as security, but instead on the proof that he has a job and a regular income. As a result, payday loans come with high-interest rates—partly because they are unsecured, and partly because they have high default rates.

Payday loan providers have been heavily criticized by some significant Christian leaders, most notably Archbishop Justin Welby, for aggressive advertising, the levels of interest charged, and aggressive collection policies. Though he rejected the option of calling for legislative bans on payday lending, Welby stated in 2013 that he wanted to push payday lenders out of business by encouraging the developments of financial cooperatives (including one managed by his own church) that would provide competition to payday lenders.[18]

Payday loans are subject to different regulations in different countries, with some nations imposing interest-rate ceilings. But even if one took the view that payday loans and associated practices should be heavily regulated or even forbidden, Booth is surely correct to note the strong likelihood that such prohibitions may have a perverse effect. They could encourage people in serious financial difficulties to lie when making loan applications to more mainstream lenders. In other instances, it may even drive some desperate people into the dark world of black markets for loans and the embrace of loan sharks who enforce failure to meet payments with brutality.[19] This is a classic instance of what economists call unintended consequences: a well-intentioned policy aimed at helping one group—in this case, often quite vulnerable people—but which can seriously hurt the same or other groups.

Regulation and Virtue

The question of financial regulation is thus more complicated than often supposed. This should make Christians think twice before

they automatically suggest that too little regulation is at the root
of our financial problems. At a minimum, Booth notes, if governments want to impose more regulation on financial systems in the
name of the common good, Christians should ask two important
questions. The first concerns cause and effect: did the problem flow
from an absence of regulation, too much regulation, or simply the
wrong type of regulation? The second question concerns regulation's
moral dimension and unintended consequences: do the problems
flow from regulations and laws that actually inhibit accountability
and transparency?[20]

Examples of financial regulation gone awry are not hard to find.
One recent instance is the 2,300-page Dodd-Frank Wall Street
Reform and Consumer Protection Act. After the financial crisis of
2008, it was politically inevitable that significant regulatory change
would occur. Writing four years after Dodd-Frank's passage through
Congress, however, the financial policy scholar Peter Wallison argued
that the legislation had introduced severe confusion into financial
regulation:

> There is always a trade-off between regulation and economic
> growth, but Dodd-Frank—by far the most intrusive and costly
> financial regulation since the New Deal—placed few if any
> limitations on regulatory power. Written broadly and leaving
> regulators to fill in the details, the act has often left regulators
> in doubt about what Congress meant. Even after regulations
> have been finalized, interpreting them can be a trial. For exam-
> ple, the regulations implementing the inconsistent Volcker
> Rule, which prohibited banks and their affiliates from trading
> securities for their own account, took more than three years to
> write, but key provisions are still unclear. . . . None of this was
> necessary. The administration and Congress acted hastily. The
> Treasury Department sent draft legislation to Congress only a
> few months after taking office in 2009, and the law—spurred
> by a promise from then-Rep. Barney Frank for a "new New
> Deal"—passed a year later.[21]

Leaving aside the economics and politics of regulation, great Christian minds have affirmed that law and legislation have a critical role in shaping a given society's moral culture. The modern financial sector isn't exempt from that general principle. But orthodox Christianity also holds that regulation is not enough for people to walk in the paths of righteousness. Lord Green put it well when he stated, "If we are to restore trust and confidence in the markets, we must therefore address what is at its root a moral question."[22] And moral problems ultimately require moral solutions.

The values embodied in financial markets will reflect the values brought to the financial industry by the people acting within them. The subprime mortgage fiasco that savaged financial markets in 2008 was the result of many factors, such as governments encouraging people to take on loans they could not really afford in the pursuance of what might be seen as sound policy goals; a failure of sound vigilance on the part of lenders; and the growth of regulatory arbitrage. But does anyone doubt that if all the various actors in the subprime-mortgage financial markets had behaved more responsibly, more prudently, and more morally, the 2008 crisis would not have been as traumatic?

In 2009, the Catholic bishops of England and Wales issued a document about the financial crisis of 2008 that reflected this careful Christian balance between the legitimacy of regulation and attention to the moral reality that if evil ultimately proceeds from within a human person, then good human choices are an indispensable part of the response. Indicating that they thought insufficient regulation was part of the problem, the bishops also suggested the crisis owed something to people putting excessive faith in markets. "Market forces," the bishops stated, "are not sovereign."[23]

The bishops were not, however, shy about stating forthrightly that the crisis reflected a broader breakdown in adherence to very basic moral principles throughout Britain—including among many British politicians and clergy.[24] Not only, they argued, had banks and investment funds lent "recklessly in the pursuit of short term profit"; but on the other side of the equation—that is, among everyday consumers of credit—there was "also the eager desire of so many to borrow beyond their means."[25]

In reflecting on such matters, we need to be attentive to evidence. It's a common assumption, for instance, that consumer credit and its widespread use are relatively new phenomena. But in America's case, for instance, the rapid growth in consumer-credit use didn't somehow explode after the deregulation of the 1980s and the spread of credit cards. The most rapid increase in the use of consumer credit actually occurred between 1945 and about 1965, after which it has generally remained stable.[26]

Whatever the facts about the use of consumer credit in Western societies, the most striking aspect of the bishops' analysis of the morally problematic uses of credit was their conclusion that they were not convinced that "new and sweeping regulation [would] of itself solve these deep seated problems." In the long term, the bishops held, Britain needed to rediscover virtues such as prudence, justice, fortitude, and temperance, underpinned by the theological virtue of charity. Unfortunately, the bishops suggested, Britain had gone in the opposite direction:

> In place of virtue we have seen an expansion of regulation. A society that is held together just by compliance to rules is inherently fragile, open to further abuses which will be met by a further expansion of regulation. This cannot be enough. The virtues are not about what one is allowed to do but who one is formed to be. They strengthen us to become moral agents, the source of our own actions. The classical virtues form us as people who are prudent, just, temperate and courageous. The Christian virtues of faith, hope and charity root our human growth in the gifts of God and form us for our ultimate happiness: friendship with God.[27]

The importance of the bishops' reflection lies less in their circumspect remarks about regulation. In no way could they be seen as opposed in principle to any expansion of regulation. Rather, their point—which should be carefully assimilated by all Christians—is that no amount of regulation of the financial industry can substitute for the living out of the virtues on the part of bankers, regulators, financial advisors, and consumers. This won't ensure that no problems or fraud will occur in the future. But apart from being good in itself, one side effect of the spread of such habits would surely be fewer of the imprudent and reckless choices that invariably contribute to financial crises.

Central Banks and Monetary Stability

Modern forms of regulating financial markets seem far removed from the manner in which medieval and early-modern governments addressed these forms of economic activity. One constant, however, between then and now in Christian reflection on this subject is the principle that the state has a responsibility for maintaining monetary stability. Writing in the twentieth century on the ethics of money, for instance, Messner stated that, from the standpoint of Christian ethics and natural law, "the maintenance of the stability of the value of money is the fundamental obligation of justice."[28]

But what does monetary stability entail? As noted in this book's introduction, monetary stability can be measured in three ways. One is the *relative value* of a currency vis-à-vis other currencies (the exchange rate). A second is the *opportunity cost* associated with the volume of money likely to be available in the future (the interest rate). The third is its *purchasing power* (the inflation rate).

Monetary instability can thus take a variety of forms. Prices can, for instance, cease to be relatively stable (e.g., inflation takes off). Unstable exchange rates can dramatically alter the competitive advantage of businesses in different countries but in ways that have nothing to do with these businesses' relative productivity levels.

While these specifics are important, the underlying significance of monetary stability lies in the way that it helps money perform its key functions. The first lesson outlined in most introductions to theories about money is that money's most basic function is to serve as a medium of exchange. From this standpoint, money serves as a proxy for the value of real goods and services that are objects of individual

economic exchange. This forms the basis of money's three other functions: a store of value, a unit of account, and a standard of deferred
payment.

These functions allow money to serve as a conveyor of information through the price system, thereby allowing a type of order to be
brought to the seemingly anarchic character of the market. As prices
increase and decline in response to consumer demand, the available
supply of goods and services, and the emergence of new and/or better products and services, the price information conveyed through
the medium of money allows resources to be constantly reallocated
to meet ever-changing needs and wants. Money thus permits a coor-
dination of millions of pieces of economic information dispersed
among billions of individuals.

If these are accepted as money's essential functions and roles, there
are strong reasons to try to ensure that the value of money is maintained at a stable level over long periods of time. As far as possible, the
supply of and the demand for money should not become detached or
operate separately from the actual supply of and demand for goods
and services (what economists call the "true" price relativities). This
in turn translates into the type of monetary policy that, first, seeks
to prevent money's functions from being corrupted by disturbances
emanating from the money supply itself, and, second, attempts to
prevent the supply of money itself from facilitating changes in the
production and distribution of goods and services.

This does not mean that anyone is capable of establishing a perfect
equilibrium between the value of money and the supply and demand
of goods and services. Some friction is inevitable, not least because of
time lags in the formation of prices. It may well be that constancy in a
given currency's average purchasing power is the best we can aim for.

A number of moral concerns underlie this position. One is an
emphasis on facilitating liberty of exchange and economic security
by reducing the uncertainty that can flow from fluctuations in the
value of money that have nothing to do with the relative valuation
of different goods and services. Constant oscillations in the value of
money undermine people's ability to discern what they find marginally preferable to what they consider marginally less preferable.

Another value at stake is the way in which stable money usually translates into greater economic prosperity for more people. As Bishop Oresme specified centuries ago, merchants will tend to go where there is monetary stability.[29] Greater monetary certainty is considered a spur to productivity and capital investment, both domestic and foreign, not least because many long-term contracts benefit from a confidence that prices will remain relatively constant over time.

Monetary Policy, the Poor, and the Wealthy

Lastly, there is a concern to which Christians should be especially attentive: the manner in which monetary stability helps particular marginalized groups. These include millions of people who lack the financial sophistication to navigate the waters of inflation, and people (such as the elderly and the disabled) on fixed incomes that aren't always indexed to inflation. Such people aren't usually in a position to invest in the stock market to maintain the value of their assets. Likewise, a salaried worker who receives a 3-percent wage increase in a given year will find the value of his raise halved by an inflation rate as low as 1.5 percent in the same year. Over the medium to long term, this makes it difficult for such income groups to maintain (let alone increase) their salaries' purchasing power.[30]

This isn't to suggest there are no instances in which central banks and/or governments can engage in currency devaluations or quantitative easing. In emergencies or highly unusual economic and political conditions, there may be a legitimate case for this.[31] Scholastic thinkers, we have seen, generally argued that there were instances in which debasements could be justified. Property *is* subordinate to the realization of the universal destination of material goods, and that includes money.

One major difference between the context of the present and that of medieval and early-modern Christian commentators is that "hard money" (whether in the form of metallic currencies or a gold standard) is not used today. That means that the intrinsic value of a currency is not dependent on the value or composition of a particular metal owned by a person, persons, or the state.

In many ways, the absence of "hard money" makes the possibility of state-induced inflation easier. And modern Christian social ethicists have traditionally taken as dim a view of using inflation to overcome economic problems as scholastic theologians took of currency debasements. Messner, for instance, underscored the economic and political damage done by inflation to entire societies in the twentieth century and the way that it contributed to the rise of totalitarian regimes in Germany and Russia.[32]

At the level of credit and debt transactions, inflation can benefit debtors economically by reducing the real amount of what they owe. From the angle of commutative justice, this is very problematic. On the other end of the equation, inflation also encourages creditors to protect themselves by building anticipated inflation into interest-rate charges as a way of recovering their losses, passing on the costs to debtors.

Beyond issues of inflation, governments can conduct monetary policy in ways that profoundly damage the common good. Excessive reliance on monetary policy to stimulate the economy instead of tackling deeper, more intractable, economic problems that may be politically unpopular to address can mean that a government is not facing up to its responsibilities to the common good.

A less-noticed impact on justice that follows from monetary policy errors concerns a particular way in which they can privilege those who are already wealthy. As the economist and scholar of Catholic social doctrine Jörg Guido Hülsmann writes, when a central bank issues excess liquidity, "the additional money benefits the first owners at the expense of all other money owners. It is true that this is so irrespective of whether the additional money results from natural production or from inflation."[33] Writing about this issue in the context of American monetary policy, the commentator Ruchir Sharma wrote six years after the 2008 financial crisis:

> Federal Reserve Chair Janet Yellen has said the central bank's goal is "to help Main Street not Wall Street." ... But talk to anyone on Wall Street. If they are being frank, they'll admit that the Fed's loose monetary policy has been one of the biggest

contributors to their returns over the past five years. . . . The
Fed can print as much money as it wants, but it can't control
where it goes, and much of it is finding its way into financial
assets. On many long-term metrics, the stock market is now at
levels that fall within the top 10% of valuations recorded over
the past 100 years. The rally in the fixed-income market too
is reaching giddy proportions, particularly for high-yield junk
bonds, which are up 150% since 2009.

It's no secret who owns most of these assets. The wealthiest
1% of households . . . now owns 50% of all financial wealth in
the U.S., and the top 10% owns 91% of the wealth in stocks
and mutual funds.[34]

In short, the wealthy are usually in a position to invest the new
money in, for instance, real estate, the stock market, works of art,
hedge funds and thus at least keep up with (or even exceed) inflation.
The less well-off and the poor, by contrast, don't have the same degree
of access to such possibilities and are in less of a position to recoup
the depreciation of their money or income.

A World Central Bank?

Modern central banking as a process for managing monetary policy is
a relatively recent phenomenon. The remit of central banks as institutions has been limited to the level of nation-states. The decisions
of some central banks—such as the Federal Reserve, the Bank of
England, the Bank of Japan, and the European Central Bank—matter more for the global economy than others. It's also the case that
central bankers have consulted one another in informal and formal
settings for decades.

Such discussions reflect the fact that we live in an increasingly globalized economy. For many people, the reality of such an economy
means that we need global financial institutions. Christians have
figured prominently in calls for such arrangements. In 2009, for
instance, Archbishop Rowan Williams suggested that "[t]he existing international instruments—the IMF and World Bank, the WTO

and the G8 and G20 countries—need to be reconceived as both monitors of the global flow of capital and agencies to stimulate local enterprise and provide some safety nets as long as the global playing field is so far from being level."[35]

Two years later, in 2011, the Note published by the Pontifical Council for Justice and Peace suggested that the statutes of the International Monetary Fund implied "the commitment to create some form of global monetary management." The Note added that "one can see an emerging requirement for a body that will carry out the functions of a kind of 'central world bank' that regulates the flow and system of monetary exchanges, as do the national central banks."[36]

The notion that an increasingly integrated world requires some type of authority able to make decisions about what some Christians call "the universal common good" has long been a staple of Catholic social doctrine as well as other expressions of Christian social ethics. But those same traditions have generally been careful never to specify the precise form that such an authority or authorities might take.[37] That is squarely an issue for lay Christians. Hence, references to a global world authority in, for instance, Catholic social teaching are invariably accompanied by an emphasis on the idea of subsidiarity. The Note specifies, for instance, that any higher-level intervention from a world authority should occur "*only when* individual, social or financial actors are intrinsically deficient in capacity, or cannot manage by themselves to do what is required of them."[38]

In principle, there is no necessary reason for Christians to object to international institutions or even some form of world authority. Within this framework, however, there is much room for legitimate disagreements about the nature and extent of any such authority's powers, including in the realm of finance. It is one thing to have forums in which central bankers and heads of government can meet to discuss and perhaps even seek to coordinate monetary policy. That could be seen as a type of exercise of authority. But if a global central bank were created and charged with setting something like a global interest rate for a global currency, then it would be effectively seeking to set a global price for capital through setting an optimal world interest rate. We must ask whether the results would be any more satisfactory than those of the adoption of the Euro. Given that the economies of the world at large are even more diverse than those within Europe, there is little reason to hope so.

Before forming their views on these questions, lay Christians should consider a number of issues. First, there is no reason to suppose that the errors made by national central banks wouldn't be replicated by a global central bank. If there is a lesson to be learned from the European Union's experience of the 2008 financial crisis, it is the problems associated with a centralized supranational body such as the European Central Bank setting a one-size-fits-all interest rate for economies as different as Greece, Ireland, and Germany.

Second, it is simply impossible for any one individual or organization to know what is the optimal interest rate for every economy in the world. It is hard enough for central banks to "guesstimate" what should be the optimal amount of credit in a national economy. Here it is worth considering an insight stressed by the economist Friedrich von Hayek in his Nobel Prize address in 1974 when reflecting on the limits of economics' predictive powers:

[T]he chief point was already seen by those remarkable anticipators of modern economics, the Spanish schoolmen of the sixteenth century, who emphasized that what they called *pretium mathematicum*, the mathematical price, depended on so many particular circumstances that it could never be known to man but was known only to God. I sometimes wish that our mathematical economists would take this to heart.[39]

Economic forecasting is a notoriously inexact exercise, despite the wealth of mathematical brain power invested in this activity. The difficulty (if not impossibility) associated with such a global institution determining a global interest rate, or single-handedly managing the world's money supply, or engaging in open-market operations on a global scale (even if armed with volumes of statistics) should be clear. It would be to ascribe such an institution with godlike qualities. And for mortals to aspire to omnipotence is folly.

Humility and a Higher Calling

Like many of the issues discussed throughout this book, the questions surrounding the creation of something like a global central bank underscore the need for Christians to approach the ethical and economic questions associated with finance with a considerable degree of humility. Certainly there are many principles derived from Christian faith, reason, and history that can assist us in bringing moral clarity to this sector of the economy. But what often seem like common sense solutions to questions ranging from compensation levels in finance to the conduct of monetary policy often raise, as we have seen, some significant questions—and not just those of an economic nature but also issues of justice.

It is important to help Christians and others in finance to adhere to the demands of moral truth so that they avoid evil and give their neighbors what they are due. This needs, however, to go hand in hand with something even more fundamental for Christians in finance that has received comparatively little attention. For the hundreds of thousands of Christians who work in finance, something more is required: a description and understanding of finance as a calling—of finance as a *vocation*.

Further Reading

Bishops' Conference of England and Wales. *Choosing the Common Good*. Stoke in Trent: Alive Publishing, 2010.

Durkin, Thomas A., Gregory Elliehausen, Michael E. Staten, and Todd J. Zywicki. *Consumer Credit and the American Economy*. Oxford: Oxford University Press, 2014.

Green, Stephen. *Good Value: Reflections on Money, Morality, and an Uncertain World*. London: Penguin Books, 2009.

Koppl, Roger. *From Crisis to Confidence*. London: IEA, 2014.

Salins, A. de, and F. Villeroy de Galhau. *Le développement moderne des activités financiers au regard des exigences éthiques du Christianisme*. Vatican City: Pontifical Council for Justice and Peace, 1994.

8

Finance as *Vocatio,* Finance as *Magnificentia*

It is not he who has many possessions that you should call blessed: he more rightly deserves that name who knows how to use the gods' gifts wisely.

Horace[1]

Expending larger incomes so that opportunity for gainful work may be abundant, provided, however, that this work is applied to producing really useful goods, ought to be considered, as We deduce from the principles of the Angelic Doctor, an outstanding exemplification of the virtue of magnificence and one particularly suited to the needs of the times.

Pius XI[2]

In recent decades, many Christians have proved more willing to articulate generally positive visions of commerce. The first significant contemporary effort to provide deeper theological grounding for business occurred when Michael Novak's *Spirit of Democratic Capitalism* was published in 1982.

Since that time commerce has generally received more favorable treatment in Christian social ethics. Even a pontiff perceived to be as critical of contemporary market economies as Pope Francis once described business as a "a noble vocation, provided that those engaged in it see themselves challenged by a greater meaning in life; this will enable them truly to serve the common good by striving to increase the goods of this world and to make them more accessible to all."[3] Among Evangelical Anglicans, scholars such as Brian Griffiths and Peter Heslam have promoted similarly positive theological visions of business.[4] All these thinkers have also been careful to condemn what's often called the "prosperity gospel" or "prosperity theology"—the idea that true Christian faith necessarily leads to an increase in one's financial and material assets.

With specific regard to finance, however, it is much harder to find extended Christian reflections in which words such as "calling" or "vocation" feature prominently. Hesitation about invoking such language may owe something to Christians' often skeptical views of the moral status of various activities associated with finance. As noted, many Christians are happy to affirm finance as a necessary, even substantial economic activity. To endow it with moral depth beyond the category of useful, however, is a step that many Christians find harder to take.

Over the centuries, Christians invested much time and energy exploring the moral challenges characterizing finance so as to help those working in finance *know how* to avoid sin. But the other half of the Christian moral life is the *choosing and doing* of the good. What follows is an effort to sketch—and no more than sketch—how Christians can think about finance as a vocation: as a particular way of living out the life of freedom and love to which Christ calls us in what some Christians no doubt regard as an unlikely portion of the Lord's vineyard. Judging from the statements of many Christians, finance lies on society's moral peripheries—perhaps even at the outer boundaries of respectability. That, however, is precisely why Christians need to be in that part of the global marketplace: to lift it out of the realm of moral ambiguity and expediency and help to transform it into a sphere in which great works can be done.

Understanding vocatio

Today the word "vocation" is used in many different contexts, some of which have little connection to Christian belief and practice. Vocation nevertheless retains a quite specific meaning in Christian faith. Derived from the Latin *vocatio*, vocation is best understood as a *summons* from the Lord himself. We have intimations of this notion of being summoned in Paul's letter to the Corinthians. "What each one has," the Apostle writes, "is what the Lord has given him and he should continue as he was when God's call reached him" (1 Cor. 7:17).

The context of this statement is Paul's reflections on marriage. Successive generations of Christians were not slow to apply the idea of being called by God to particular tasks that, in their specific ways, help to build up the Kingdom of God. The writings of Aquinas, for instance, indicate that he believed that the very nature of human society meant that different people were destined to fulfill different tasks.[5]

The Reformation provided particular stimulus to Christian thought about the notion of vocation. New and dynamic Catholic religious orders such as the Jesuits stressed the need for people to regard their diverse occupations as a calling from God.[6] Similar notions were present in Protestant thought. "For Calvin," the Evangelical Anglican scholar Alister McGrath points out, "God places individuals where He wants them to be."[7]

At the same time, the idea of vocation was not reduced to a person's precise profession. In his *Treatise of the Vocations or Callings of Men*, for instance, the Puritan theologian William Perkins (1558–1602) subordinated people's particular vocations to the realization of the Christian's broader calling to salvation and witnessing to God's glory.[8] Likewise, one of the most influential Protestant professions of faith of the time, the Westminster Confession, clearly distinguished between a person's heavenly and earthly callings. Christians, the Confession emphasizes, should ensure that their earthly responsibilities don't distract them from pursuing their heavenly destiny. It also stresses that Christians should choose "that employment or calling in which you may be most serviceable to God. Choose not that in which you may be most honorable in the world; but that which you may do most good and best escape sinning."[9]

At the most basic level, Christianity teaches that every person is summoned to choose Christ, and to *change* one's life and free choices accordingly. The Orthodox theologian Father Thomas Hopko puts it this way: "In a certain sense every person has the same vocation, which is to be a saint. We are all called to be saints, to be holy as God is holy, to be perfect as the Father in heaven is perfect." In this sense, Hopko notes, *every* Christian's vocation is religious.[10] Striving for holiness isn't limited to those who are called to be ordained ministers or the religious life. As one twentieth-century saint, Josemaría Escrivá, wrote, "In order to reach sanctity, an ordinary Christian— who is not a religious [i.e., called to life in a monastery or convent]— has no reason to abandon the world, since that is precisely where he is to find Christ."[11]

At the core of the Christian's vocation to be holy is living a life of love. The *Catechism of the Catholic Church* goes so far as to state, "Love is the fundamental and innate vocation of every human being."[12] Christian love isn't of course mere sentimentalism in which Christ is reduced to a therapeutic teddy bear. Nor is life in Christ about embracing politically correct, fashionable causes. One of the ways we live out the Christian call to sanctity is to consistently choose the truths of the narrow way revealed by Christ that direct us toward human flourishing and away from the inner disintegration that occurs whenever we choose to sin. Why else would Christians, from the very beginning, have sought to apply the demands of Christian morality knowable through faith and reason to every aspect of their lives?

We all know people who appear not to have identified their particular calling in life and, as a result, seem lost in the world and often in considerable spiritual distress. The question of vocation, in fact, boils down to this: How should I live out the general Christian vocation in the specifics of my time and in light of my particular gifts and opportunities? Thus, I don't decide to follow a particular profession because it "feels right" for me. Rather, knowing one's vocation involves discerning the particular path specifically willed for us by God but which the Lord also gives us the freedom to embrace. In that sense, following a vocation means (1) identifying what God has in mind for a person through discernment, prayer, and consultation and (2) freely conforming one's choices to God's specific plan.

Both stages are important. Once a person is relatively confident that *this path* rather than other possible options is his calling, he must begin the work of providing himself with the knowledge and skills to live out his vocation and in ways consistent with Christian faith and morals.

Making Money Good

How might we begin to outline the specifics of the vocation of the person who discerns that he is called to work in the financial sector? A somewhat paradoxical starting point may be found in Pope Francis's *Evangelii Gaudium*. This text is full of the type of provocative queries typically asked by old-style Jesuit preachers to help listeners examine their consciences. Few of Francis's questions, however, were more provocative than the following: "How can it be that it is not a news item when an elderly homeless person dies of exposure, but it is news when the stock market loses two points?"[13]

Such a question should make anyone pause and wonder just how much our attention to the world's financial ups and downs may have blinded us to the raw suffering of those in whom Christ tells us we see his face. Every day the world's newspapers are full of prognostications about global financial markets. It's rare, however, for news about the very tangible sufferings of the some of the least among us—the unborn, those crushed by addictions, the aged with no one to care for them, abandoned children—happening right in front of us to push financial commentary to the back pages.

There are, however, good reasons for Christians to be concerned about, for instance, significant drops in the Dow Jones Index, the FTSE 100, the Nasdaq, the DAX, or the CAC 40, if only because such numbers have a major impact on how many people—how many unique, irreplaceable images of God—will indeed suffer loss of jobs, have trouble feeding their families, and otherwise become the very poor who deserve our care. To the extent these are gauges of investor confidence or investor sentiment concerning hundreds of thousands of large and small businesses as well as numerous economic opportunities in a given market, their fluctuations tell us something about the likelihood of the overall sum of wealth increasing or decreasing in a given society over the near, medium, and long term.

If, for instance, the stock market undergoes a slow but steady decline in value, this is an indication that the economy is not performing especially well. And that decline in value and investor confidence diminishes a society's ability over time to grow the resources we need to facilitate many forms of human flourishing (employment being a notable illustration) but which also help reduce the odds of elderly people dying alone in the streets. In short, a diminished financial sector can translate into diminished material resources to help our neighbor in need. Material resources aren't everything with regard to helping those in need. But they aren't nothing.

More generally, when finance's ability to perform its particular functions starts to degrade, it becomes harder for a society to promote the universal destination of material goods over extended periods of time. From this standpoint, a specific dimension of the vocation of those who work in finance is to realize what might be called the *goodness of money*.

That's an expression many Christians may find quite jarring. Yet when we look at authoritative sources such as Scripture and the Church Fathers, nowhere do we find the claim that using money is intrinsically evil. Instead it is presented as an *instrument*—one that, to be sure, can distract people from their primary call to conform their lives and choices to Christ, but one also capable of being used for good.

In *What Your Money Means*, Frank Hanna argues that we need to wake up and realize that "money is good." Hanna isn't hawking some type of prosperity gospel. Nor is Hanna suggesting that money is a good as fundamental to human flourishing as goods such as life, beauty, friendship, or work. Rather, Hanna's point is that money's very nature is such that it can be quickly redirected toward helping to realize the good: not just the creation of other instrumental goods but also those goods that are core to who we are as human beings made in the *imago Dei*.

Insofar as finance is about what might be called the engineering of money in the form of capital, it has immense potential to contribute to the common good and therefore human flourishing. Money, Hanna points out, enables us to employ people (and thus promote work), build hospitals (and therefore promote life), and create companies (and thereby facilitate human creativity and relationships). Money, argues Hanna, "gives us power over resources—material and human. It gives us the power to direct the development, management, consumption, and disposition of resources."[14]

Or, to make the same point negatively: Imagine a world in which capital formation was either very weak or nonexistent—where we had chosen, in effect, to "burn" all our money. The result would most likely be an economy in which the vast majority of people would be very poor and unable to become socially mobile. In such a world, it would be extremely difficult for people to make long-term savings, obtain credit on an affordable scale, buy houses, start businesses, sustain large-scale enterprises that employ thousands over long periods of time, or for individuals and businesses in developing nations to grow their way out of poverty with the assistance of injections of capital from the developed world and international financial markets. Debt, to the extent it existed, would become identified with poverty and meeting consumption needs. We would be back in the type of economy that existed before the financial revolution of the Middle Ages.

A world obsessed with finance is a very unhappy world. But so too would be a world without finance—at least for most people. "Burning money," Hanna notes, "squanders the power it gives us to shape our lives and those of others. Burning money shrinks opportunities, limits choices, and leaves us more vulnerable to the whims of time and chance and circumstances."[15] Those in the business of finance who make mistakes can seriously undermine the well-being of the poor, the aged, and others living on society's outskirts and undermine some of the conditions that help all to flourish. Yet without finance and those skilled in financial engineering, we face the prospect of largely subsistence economies and dramatically reduced opportunities for human flourishing. We would also live in societies in which the very same marginalized people would have even more diminished prospects for escaping poverty, while those with more wealth would also have fewer economic resources to help those in need.

Building Trust, Pricing Risk, Enabling Opportunity

Clearly the responsibilities and vocation of those who work in financial markets aren't limited to fulfilling one's contractual obligations. That, however, doesn't mean that financial actors can relegate these to a fourth-level concern. The requirements of commutative justice alone make it clear that the concrete responsibilities freely assumed by financiers to their clients, whether detailed in a contract or not, are in fact a first-order priority. The good news is that fulfilling these obligations is generally compatible with bolstering the common good.

This is especially true with regard to realizing the universal destination of material goods. Finance, we have seen, contributes to this through:

- establishing links between the economic present and economic future of individuals and communities;
- managing risk and developing methods for continually enhancing the management of risk over the short, medium, and long term; and
- creating economic value by enabling money to assume the characteristics of capital.

None of these functions are exercises in radical individualism. Finance can certainly help make us independent, but it also increases and is a sign of humans' *interdependence*. Without people, companies and institutions willing to invest *in* each other, sell financial products and services *to* each other, take risks *on* others' endeavors, loan *to* and borrow *from* each other, or speculate on the products and services produced *by* others, there would be no financial markets. There is no reality to financial markets outside or beyond these *relationships*.

One contribution that finance can thus make to the common good is to establish relationships of trust and confidence in a variety of settings. Banks and finance are such an everyday part of life that we forget about the ways in which they help to build up and sustain important forms of human interaction, most notably between the holders of capital and those who use the capital. On a very mundane level, banks provide any number of services, including payment systems within communities, money transfers, and overdrafts. Without any of these services, our economies would be far less productive than they presently are.

Building trust in this sphere is far from easy. At the best of times, most of us are reluctant to entrust our resources to those we really don't know. Part of the core activity of those who work in finance is to help establish confidence in others throughout the economy by making determinations about the likely success or failure of thousands of ideas, initiatives, and businesses.

Of course, while risk can be managed, no investment is risk free. Finance cannot eliminate risk. Nor can it guarantee that the results of risk taking will be the most optimal. Risk is risk, and no risk assessment can tell the whole story or predict the future with 100 percent accuracy.

Yet despite this inherent limitation, finance's particular ability to build trust allows it to contribute to the common good in two ways. First, people working in finance can warn others off from schemes that they judge as excessively risky for investors in light of their assessment of the needs, responsibilities, and assets of such investors. Ultimately investors must make their own choices. But a basic application of the Golden Rule—do unto others as they would do unto you—indicates that investors must be given very clear counsel about what is likely to happen.

Second, and on a positive note, finance's capacity to foster trust by guiding risk taking helps create greater economic opportunities for millions of people. Part of the genius of finance is the way that it puts to work the whole logic of *priced risk* through which an individual or company can look at their assets, make a reasonable calculation of the basis of genuine probabilities, engage in a comparison of possibilities, and thereby maximize the opportunities for successful risk taking while reducing the possibility of failure. This contributes to the creation of new jobs, new and better products, and enhanced living standards for large segments of the population. But, crucially, it also facilitates the growth of even more of the fuel that allows the economy to achieve these ends more or less continuously.

Growing Capital

In one of his many exhortations to Christians to take seriously their concrete obligations to those in material stress, St. Ambrose of Milan famously insisted, "It is the hungry man's bread that you withhold, the naked man's cloak you store away. The money you bury in the earth is the price of the poor man's ransom and freedom."[16]

These words are usually interpreted as an exhortation to be generous and to give to the poor—and not just from our surplus wealth. That is an accurate understanding. Alongside this, however, the reference to burying one's wealth in the earth—which can be viewed as an allusion to the parable of the talents—may be regarded as a warning against hoarding one's resources instead of using them in ways that benefit everyone. This goes far beyond simply giving our surplus wealth to others. Indeed, the Gospel parable to which Ambrose refers is one where a master rebukes his servant for failing to invest his money fruitfully.

In his book on Christianity and entrepreneurship, Father Tony Percy illustrates the manner in which greed, accompanied by fear, can discourage those who already possess wealth from contributing to the increased growth of wealth throughout a given society. Reflecting on the sin of love of money, Percy comments:

> [I]f a man does not moderate his love for money, it would be highly unlikely that he would embark on a great and lofty undertaking. Motivated by an inordinate love for money, the immoderate man opts for a safer form of investment that would ensure returns and the protection of his original sum. No great projects would be undertaken as a result of his love

for comfort and fear of risk. It is only the magnificent man, the man with the virtue of fortitude and a moderate love for money, who is capable of undertaking risks that will benefit the common good.[17]

Greed, these words remind us, can result in excessive economic caution, just as the "lazy servant" who buried the money entrusted to him did so because of fear.

At some point, individuals and businesses need to put their capital to work. The role played by modern finance in that connection is indispensable. But as Lord Green writes, finance's responsibility goes beyond this. Even more fundamentally, the job of finance is to maximize value that lasts.[18]

One of the few twentieth-century Christians exercising a significant position of leadership in the global church to underscore this point was Pope Pius XII. In a little-known address to Italian bankers in 1950, the pope distinguished between avarice, on the one hand, and the growing of wealth, on the other. Significantly, he did so by commenting on the parable of the talents and contrasting the risk taking and willingness to invest of the good and faithful servant with the passiveness of the fearful servant.[19] But in doing so, as Percy points out, Pius displayed "an acute awareness of the value of money." In Percy's estimation, this may well have been "the first time that a pope has acknowledged its value."[20] Making money productive is, according to Pius, one of finance's essential social contributions to the common good:

> Does not the social function of the bank consist in making it possible for the individual to render his money fruitful, even if only in small degree, instead of dissipating it, or leaving it sleep without any profit, either to himself or to others? That is why the services which a bank can render are so numerous: to facilitate and encourage savings; to preserve savings for the future, at the same time rendering them productive in the present; to enable savings to share in useful enterprises which could not be launched without them; to make as simple and

easy as possible the regulation of accounts, exchanges, commerce between the State and private organisms and, in a word, the entire economic life of the people.[21]

Few Christians today, it must be said, have *ever* heard their pastors speak in such terms about finance.

A year later in an address entitled "Function of Banking" (October 24, 1951), Pope Pius expanded on his outline of finance's vocation by portraying it as a type of intersection for economic life. "You mark," he told the assembled bankers, "the crossroads where capital, ideas and labor encounter each other."[22]

In one sense, Pius was referring to the manner in which people working in finance must think through questions such as the worth of an idea, the degree of risk involved, how much capital should be invested at what interest rate in order to calibrate the risk appropriately, and the talents, strengths, and weaknesses of those managing the proposed or existing enterprise. But Pius also had in mind the way in which finance is an arena in which new ideas are *integrated* with capital in ways that facilitate an increase in economic growth, employment, and social well-being more generally:

> [I]t seems superfluous to speak of the immediate result of the meeting of capital and ideas. In proportion to the importance of the capital and the practical value of the idea, the labor crisis will be more or less slowed up. The conscientious and hardworking laborer will find employment more easily; the growth of production will progressively, though perhaps slowly, lead toward an economic balance; the many inconveniences and disorders, deplorably resulting from strikes, will be lessened for the greater good of a healthy domestic, social and moral life.[23]

Pius also proved willing to drill down into some of the very specific realties that people in finance encounter every day. "A young inventor," he told his audience, "a man with initiative, a benefactor of humanity comes to you for a loan. You must study him in order not to put the trusting lender into the hands of a utopian or crook, in order to avoid the risk of sending away a deserving borrower capable of giving immense services but merely lacking the necessary funds for carrying them out."[24]

Once again, however, Pius emphasizes that the point of this type of scrutiny is to make capital productive so that it can help build up many of the conditions that make up the common good:

> How much capital is lost through waste and luxury, through selfish and dull enjoyment, or accumulates and lies dormant without being turned to profit! There will always be egoists and self-seekers; there will always be misers and those who are shortsightedly timid. Their number could be considerably reduced if one could interest those who have money in using their funds wisely and profitably, be they great or small. It is largely due to this lack of interest that money lies dormant. You can remedy this to a great extent by making ordinary depositors collaborators, either as bond or share-holders, in undertakings whose launching and thriving would be of great benefit to the community, such as industrial activities, agricultural production, public works, or the construction of houses for workers, educational or cultural institutions, welfare or social services.[25]

Note that Pius is not simply talking about the capital of the wealthy. Finance, to his mind, is a way of making *everyone's* capital fruitful. It does so by drawing people *out of themselves* and their immediate preoccupations by helping to establish and widen the range of possibilities for both holders and seekers of capital. In this way, finance mobilizes capital in new and effective ways, highlights alternative uses of the same capital, and helps people from all backgrounds make assessments of what they want to buy and sell in any number of ventures in light of how much or how little risk they want to undertake. Modern finance thus helps give effect to man's economic creativity, freedom, and interdependence in ways once largely beyond most people.

Credit, the Poor, and Loving Our Neighbor

Though financial markets are now accessible to previously unimaginable numbers of people, it's also the case that millions still find it hard to enter the same markets in even remote ways. For many people, credit is not about access to the fuel for economic opportunity. It is about making ends meet, much as it was before the medieval financial revolution.

Love and action for the poor—the materially, morally, and spiritually poor—is as much part of the vocation of the Christian in finance as it is for any other Christian. But how does living out the Christian option for the poor fit into the particularities of a vocation in finance?

At a minimum, one significant responsibility of Christians is to think seriously about how to ensure that finance does not exploit or marginalize the poor. This involves being clear minded about the discernible and measurable effects of different proposals for helping those in need. Some of these proposals, no matter how well intentioned, may actually harm the poor. Recall, for instance, an issue we touched on in Chapter 6: proposals for caps on interest rates.

Though interest-rate caps have often been employed as a way to prevent vulnerable people from getting into severe financial difficulties, the evidence indicates that they are not very effective. Looking at the case of payday loans in 2012, Philip Booth pointed out:

> France and Germany, which both have interest rate caps, had around five times the level of complete financial breakdown—such as bankruptcy—among people who had trouble with their debts. While the figure stood at only 4 percent in the UK, in France and Germany it was between 20 and 25 percent. This is a shocking statistic. Financial breakdown of this kind is often accompanied by difficulties in obtaining housing, employment and the purchase of essentials such as food.[26]

It also turns out that the number of those tapping into the black market for loans—which involves truly usurious interest rates and is often characterized by the use of violence to enforce payment—is much less in Britain than in France and Germany.[27]

A better way for Christians to widen access to credit and capital for those in need is to model what the Franciscans did in the fourteenth century when they started the *montes pietatis*. To a certain extent, the microfinance movement in which Christians have played a prominent role is one modern expression of this activity. One caveat is that such institutions should avoid any paternalism, such as attempting to micromanage a borrower's use of the capital. To flourish, people need to make free choices for the good, including in finance.

This leads us to another caution. Strategies and instruments such as microfinance are good but should be seen as a way of facilitating the entry of individuals and companies into more regular ways of accessing capital and credit rather than as a permanent state of affairs. Getting from absolute poverty to relative poverty is a good start. But it is *only* a first start if poverty is to be systematically addressed.

Another issue that financial actors must navigate when living out concern for the poor is how to help those whose poverty is not material but rather moral and spiritual, such as the person who uses credit to fuel a gambling addiction. Addressing these often very complicated matters requires us to reflect on a number of related issues. How free do we allow transactions between financial institutions and their clients to be? How do we hold people accountable for their free choices? How far can we go to protect people from self-destructive behaviors? Above all, what does it mean to love our neighbor in such circumstances? It would, for instance, be foolish for a financial institution to ignore signs of trouble in a loan, and it should certainly act swiftly in cases of fraud. At the same time, it is not the bank's responsibility to meddle in the details of the client's legitimate use of borrowed capital.

The commandment to love our neighbor, however, means that Christians in finance have obligations that exceed these parameters. It is not paternalistic, for instance, for a banker to tell a client that his investment choices are seriously endangering his family's financial security. If the same customer refuses to change behavior, an investment advisor may have to decline to continue acting as a conduit for resources that enable the client to act irresponsibly. Nor should a Christian in the financial sector hesitate to point such clients in the direction of those capable of addressing the deeper problems often at the root of financial irresponsibility. The client may need a psychiatrist or a pastor more than a banker. This doesn't amount to an abandonment of care for the client on the financier's part. It's a matter of identifying *who* has the capacity to deal with particular questions. Monitoring fraud and deception is something that financial institutions can and already do. But they aren't the best first responders to any number of other social pathologies.[28]

What Christians in finance can do is ask searching questions about what drives many people to misuse credit—questions that invariably point to problems that go far beyond finance. An example of how to do this was provided by Pope Benedict XVI in 2010. When asked about the recourse to high levels of private and public debt by individuals, businesses, and governments in developed nations, Benedict wisely declined to enter into the economic debates concerning whether high public debt and deficit spending boosts or undermines long-term economic growth. Instead, he pointed to deeper moral challenges that may, at least in part, help explain the apparent addiction to debt in many Western nations.

In the first place, he argued, the readiness of so many individuals and governments to take on such high amounts of debt may mean that "we are living at the expense of future generations."[29] If that is true, then such borrowing constitutes a rather blatant violation of intergenerational solidarity. Even more fundamentally, however, the pope suggested that the choice to use debt so frequently was symptomatic of a wider and deeper problem—that people were "living in untruth." "We live," Benedict commented, "on the basis of appearances, and the huge debts are meanwhile treated as something that we are simply entitled to."[30] Here Benedict pointed beyond the questions of justice that have traditionally preoccupied many Christians reflecting on finance. Instead, he touched on how our use of capital reflects our more general attitude toward material goods and the way it embodies—or undermines—our choice to live our lives in the ways that Christ calls us to do.

Debt and the Developing World

The consumerism and living for now often associated with the misuse of debt and capital is very much associated with developed nations. The financial challenges faced by the poor in developing nations are often quite different.

The debts owed by many such countries to Western private banks and governments are one such issue. As previously discussed, debt in the form of bonds and securities has been a means by which governments have raised capital to realize many projects, especially from the eleventh century onward. Some such goals, such as the development of public infrastructure, have merit because they genuinely serve the social and economic dimensions of the common good.

Looking, however, at the poverty prevailing in, for instance, many African nations, many Christians have called for debt forgiveness for the governments of such countries. How, they ask, can Western banks and governments possibly require developing nations to continue paying interest on loans that are often decades old and on which the principal has often been paid many times over? Don't such interest payments result in less capital being available for these governments to address poverty in their societies? Looking for scriptural precedents for such action, many Christians have pointed to the Jubilee year in ancient Israel. This required cancellation of debts. Why should the same principle not be applied to cases such as heavily indebted developing nations?

As with most such cases, a one-size-fits-all approach to this issue is likely to gloss over some important distinctions. In certain instances, there may be grounds for Christians to press for debt forgiveness. In the 1950s, 1960s, and 1970s, many Western governments, international financial institutions, and private banks loaned capital to regimes that they *knew* to be tyrannical and highly corrupt. To the degree that extending credit to such regimes involved an element of cooperation with such injustices, Western public and private financial actors are culpable. And justice demands some form of restitution.

It follows that financial actors concerned with being just should assess the extent to which they were complicit in what's referred to as "odious debt." This expression is used to describe the advancement of credit to regimes that, at the time of the making of such loans, could have been reasonably assessed as having no interest in investing the capital to promote the nation's common good and even intent on using the money for corrupt purposes.

The situation, however, is complicated by the fact that many of the regimes that negotiated the original odious debt have been succeeded by legitimate governments. The question thus arises: Should the responsibility for past odious debt be passed on to the legitimate successors of tyrannical and corrupt regimes? Under international law, the principle governing such situations is that the state, as the embodiment of national sovereignty, holds liability for such debt. This liability is passed on from one government to the next.

In general, there are good reasons why this principle should continue to be followed. First, violation of this principle could conceivably set a precedent that allows governments to repudiate a previous government's debts simply because they didn't agree with the loans. That would produce chaos in global financial markets. Second, repudiation of the loan damages the nation's common good by undermining its international creditworthiness and hence access to foreign capital. As Hülsmann states, "Responsible governments can obtain loans on the free market, and in fact do obtain such loans all the time. Poverty of the nation is not an obstacle."[31] What often is a barrier to accessing capital is the lack of confidence that governments will pay back their loans.

Fiscally irresponsible governments, Hülsmann comments, are also the type of regimes that tend to obtain "political credit" through organizations such as the IMF and the World Bank.[32] The worst offenders in terms of loaning money to corrupt regimes have not been private financial actors but international governmental financial authorities. These institutions' record regarding loans to countries ranging from the Philippines under Ferdinand Marcos to Zaire under the Mobutu regime is not distinguished. Hülsmann correctly notes that such loans often helped "keep corrupt and irresponsible governments in business longer than they otherwise would be."[33]

What, however, of loans of capital to developing nations that weren't odious but were mismanaged or expended on policies and projects that failed? Here it is more questionable whether justice demands that Western governments and banks are obliged to forgive such debt. Mistakes or mismanagement are not reasons in themselves for such forgiveness.

But doesn't the Christian emphasis on mercy require us to go beyond justice? That is surely true. But mercy does not require us to blind ourselves to the entirely foreseeable effects of particular actions. Some Christians may not, for instance, have fully considered the very predictable damage done by outright and condition-free forgiveness of nonodious debt to a developing nation's creditworthiness. Failure to make interest payments or to pay back the principal of a loan undercuts a nation's creditworthiness just as much as it affects an individual's. It follows that extending mercy in these conditions would be better realized through a renegotiation—even a generous renegotiation—of the original debts and interest payment schedule.

In the past, many banks sought to protect themselves against loan defaults from governments by taking out appropriate insurance. This is a prudent way for banks to protect those who have entrusted their capital to them. But such policies can be abused. An example would be a bank that loans money to a developing nation's government in the full knowledge that the government will likely default, but judges that the guaranteed insurance payment in the event of default provides sufficient incentive to make the loan.

Such actions may be legal. Their justice is questionable. They involve a choice to make a loan to an individual or group considered highly unlikely to pay it back. Even though such a government has freely undertaken to meet the conditions of the loan, it is unfair to offer a loan to someone who doesn't have the reasonable possibility—or sometimes intention—of repaying.

It may well be that the best way for Christians in finance to assist the poor in developing nations is to look beyond granting loans to governments. Poverty alleviation certainly requires access to global capital markets on the part of individuals, businesses, and governments in developing nations. But capital will not flow to these countries in sufficient quantities over the long term unless the right institutional structures are in place: the most important being monetary stability (in all its fullness), rule of law, and protections for property rights. To that extent, Christians shouldn't be afraid to point out that anyone interested in reducing poverty through the use of capital should be at least equally attentive to the institutional prerequisites for that capital's most effective and efficient use.

One critique of such a response is that this type of institutional transformation is difficult, doesn't happen overnight, and won't necessarily address the immediate situation. This is all true. But it doesn't absolve Christians from working for long-term change, or excuse them from embarking on well-intentioned projects that may provide short-term help but that also corrode the prospects for long-term development.

In this light, one way for Christians in finance to live out their commitment to the poor would be to expend time and energy trying to develop financial instruments that can help people to escape absolute poverty in situations where basic institutional frameworks for growth aren't in place or extremely weak. Many very intelligent and creative people work in finance. They ought to be capable of finding some ways of circumventing this problem to the extent that such circumvention is possible.

Greed, Virtue, and Life in Christ

We began this book with statements from prominent Christians who have forcefully reiterated Christian teaching concerning the folly of turning money into an idol. Greed involves an inordinate attraction to something that can never ultimately satisfy us. Once greed becomes rooted in our hearts, it distorts our vision of everything and radiates outward to corrupt everything else we do in our lives. But is greed the most significant problem facing finance?

Undoubtedly greed is a part of the picture. Yet it's arguable that Christians who focus almost exclusively on greed when thinking through the challenges associated with finance may be offering an incomplete critique that overlooks some of the more significant problems characterizing modern finance. Brian Griffiths alludes to this when he reflects on some of the personality traits of those who choose finance as their career path:

> Of course some bankers are greedy. . . . But in my experience the defining characteristic of bankers is not greed; it is the ambition to be the best at what they do, to be the top of the league table, to give the best advice to clients, to execute transactions flawlessly, to provide first class research, to achieve the best returns on assets under management. When pursued to the exclusion of all else and without regard to God, this too is an idol. When it is not pursued in this way, it is a service to the common good and an important contribution to creating prosperity and reducing poverty.[34]

Combating greed in the financial sector matters. But just as important for finance's reputation and its capacity to serve the common good is *an embrace of the virtues*.

This was well understood by many bankers in the past. A good example is the founders of Barclays Bank. In more recent decades, Barclays has found itself embroiled in a number of controversies, ranging from loans to Mugabe's Zimbabwe to the Libor scandal. This is very far removed indeed from Barclays' humble beginnings.

Founded in 1690 by Quakers, much of Barclays' initial success was derived from its integration into the often-persecuted Quaker community's business activities. Looking, however, to Barclays' long-term sustainability, one of its Quaker founders, John Freame (1669–1745), was very clear that moral rather than monetary capital was the key to success. Thinking about the next generation of bankers, Freame insisted that the present generation's primary responsibility was "[t]o implant in (young) minds a sense of piety and virtue, and to train them up in the best things. This would prove more advantageous to children than getting a great deal of riches for them."[35]

In our world, many imagine that, with enough management and technological capacity, there is little we cannot achieve. The truth, however, is that even the best thought-out financial strategy, institutions, and vehicles depend at some level on people willing to live a moral life. People who lie, cheat, steal, or consistently act imprudently in finance do grave damage to the financial sector's ability to contribute to the common good. Incentives matter, institutional design is important, and some processes are better than others. Nonetheless, the sound functioning of finance ultimately relies on the choices and actions of those who work in finance, especially given their proven ability to turn most regulations to their advantage.

No less than the founder of modern economics, Adam Smith, understood that market economies need to be immersed in a culture of virtues. Self-interest, even rational self-interest, isn't enough. As his life drew to a close, Smith added a new section entitled "Of the Character of Virtue" to the sixth and final edition of his *Theory of Moral Sentiments*, published in 1790. The first edition of this book was written seventeen years before his more famous *Wealth of Nations* (1776). Smith's reasons for making this addition to the *Theory of Moral Sentiments* may never be fully known. But perhaps Smith understood that as capitalism began to spread across the globe, fueled by banks based in London and Amsterdam, people needed to be reminded that the "moral capital" that facilitates the workings of commerce, industry, and finance needed to come from somewhere "outside" the market.

It would be wrong to describe Smith as a Christian. He did, however, recognize that virtues like keeping promises, temperance, thrift, truthfulness, and humility are indispensable for the workings of modern economies. These virtues—especially prudence—serve to moderate our tendency to focus single-mindedly on our immediate reward. The prudent man in Smith's *Theory of Moral Sentiments* excels at considering his own long-term interests rather than simply short-term goals. He thus avoids excessive risk and foolish behavior in the marketplace.

Yet Smith didn't believe that there was anything especially noble about the prudent merchant. Prudence is a type of master virtue, but it isn't enough for the good life. It can also degenerate into excessive caution and fear of risk. Hence, to supplement prudence, Smith argued for the need for the emerging world of commerce to embrace and uphold the virtue of *magnanimity*.

Magnanimity, as described by Plato, Aristotle, and the Stoics, was perhaps the highest of virtues in the ancient world. For them, magnanimity is characteristic of the great-souled man who isn't afraid of risk and who often chooses to do that which is good simply because it is the noble thing to do. In the ancient world, magnanimity was associated with courageous soldiers and far-seeing statesmen—but not the merchant, of whom, as observed, the ancient world did not have an especially high view. To that extent, magnanimity seems foreign to the world of commerce.

This, however, wasn't Adam Smith's view. The prudent and virtuous man, he argued in his *Theory of Moral Sentiments*, through his "habitual and thorough conviction"[36] that God has ordered the world in particular ways and that he has placed him in a particular position for reasons "necessary for the whole," will "not only with humble resignation . . . submit to this allotment, but . . . endeavor to embrace it with alacrity and joy." It is this enthusiasm and joy that impels wise and prudent people in commercial societies to fulfill the responsibilities of the "splendid and honorable station" that God has assigned them, and consequently make "the noblest exertion which it is possible for man to make."[37]

Here Smith's language of enthusiasm and joy moves him beyond a purely Stoic view of man and into, as the philosopher Ryan Patrick Hanley has convincingly argued, the realm of Christian virtue and benevolence.[38] A parallel exists here with the citation from Pius XI referenced at the beginning of this chapter and its attention to the virtue of *magnificentia*: magnificence—a word that Pius drew explicitly from Thomas Aquinas.

Reading Aquinas's reflections on this matter is eye-opening. He defines magnificence as the virtue of "that which is great in the use of money."[39] It is not so much, he specifies, about making gifts or charity. Nor, Aquinas adds, does the person who embraces this virtue "intend principally to be lavish towards himself."[40] Rather, he says, magnificence concerns "some great work which has to be produced" with (1) a view to the good that goes beyond the immediate gain, and

(2) which cannot be done "without expenditure or outlay" of great sums of money. Moreover, magnificence for Aquinas also concerns "expenditure in reference to *hope*, by attaining to the difficulty, not simply, as magnanimity does, but in a determinate matter, namely expenditure."[41]

Here, one may speculate, we find a hitherto underappreciated basis for a Christian understanding of finance as a vocation. *Magnificentia* isn't so much about who owns the wealth. As Aquinas specifies, the poor man can also choose to do great things.[42] Rather, it is about the one who *deploys* great sums to help realize a "great work." Observe, moreover, how Aquinas links the act of magnificence to one of the three great theological virtues: the act of hope. This is especially relevant to finance, for without hope—the expectation of, and firm confidence in, positive outcomes, even in conditions of uncertainty—the entire world of finance would slowly crumble from within.

The ultimate purpose of the Christian vocation isn't to provide social lubrication to the economy. It is to speak of the revelation of Christ, bring people to faith in the same Christ, and to help fulfill the Kingdom of Christ, which will be fully realized only at the end of time. The financial sector isn't, however, excluded from this process of redemption. "There is not a square inch," wrote the Calvinist theologian Abraham Kuyper, "in the whole domain of our human existence over which Christ, who is Sovereign over all, does not cry, Mine!"[43]

Today, many believe that Christianity and contemporary finance live in entirely different worlds. To the extent that a separation exists, it is often fueled by an ignorance of finance on many Christians' part, but also a financial sector that generally doesn't (like much of our world) know how much it owes to the civilization and understanding of the world which was decisively shaped by Judaism and Christianity.

Christians certainly must do more to understand finance before rendering judgment on its workings and practitioners. To fail to do so is not only unjust; it also weakens our capacity to speak credibly about the moral dimension of finance. And that matters because finance is in as much need of the light of Christ and biblical wisdom as any other dimension of human life. As an industry with great potential for *magnificentia* by providing and calibrating in ever more sophisticated ways the great sums of capital needed by so many as they seek to make real their hopes, finance requires the presence of the religious and cultural formation that, more than any other, places hope at the very center of its vision of humanity and its future. The point is not to create "Judeo-Christian finance" or Christian investment houses, as legitimate as such enterprises may be. Instead it is to act as salt and light. The ensuing profit of a financial sector permeated by men and women inspired by the gospel is far more than the growth and effective deployment of capital, as important as it is. The ultimate yield lies in knowing—and then showing to others—how life in finance *can* be an opportunity to conform ourselves freely to the Truth, a means of serving our neighbors, and a vehicle for realizing some degree of justice in an imperfect world by helping to direct the goods of this world to their universal end: the service of humanity, which in itself helps to build up the Kingdom of God.

And this surely is where the ultimate profit worth having is finally to be found.

Endnotes

1. *Introduction*

1. Pope Francis, "Address to the New Non-Resident Ambassadors to the Holy See: Kyrgyzstan, Antigua and Barbuda, Luxembourg and Botswana," May 16, 2013. http://www.vatican.va/holy_father/francesco/speeches/2013/may/documents/papa-francesco_20130516_nuovi-ambasciatori_en.html.

2. Cited in John Carr, "Francis Puts Usury into Mix of Social Justice Concerns," *National Catholic Reporter*, January 29, 2014, http://ncronline.org/blogs/ncr-today/francis-puts-usury-mix-social-justice-concerns.

3. Pope Francis, "Money Helps, Covetousness Kills," October 21, 2013, http://www.vatican.va/holy_father/francesco/cotidie/2013/en/papa-francesco-cotidie_20131021_money-covetousness_en.html.

4. Pope Francis, "To Representatives of the Confederation of Cooperatives," February 28, 2015, http://w2.vatican.va/content/francesco/it/speeches/2015/february/documents/papa-francesco_20150228_conf cooperative.html.

5. Pius XI, *Quadragesimo anno* (1931) [hereafter QA], no. 109, no. 106, http://www.vatican.va/holy_father/pius_xi/encyclicals/documents/hf_p-xi_enc_19310515_quadragesimo-anno_en.html.

6. Archbishop John Sentamu, "Speech to the Worshipful Company of International Bankers Dinner," September 24, 2008, www.archbishopofyork.org/articles.php/1398/speech-to-the-worshipful-company-of-international-bankers-dinner.

7. For a more detailed description of short-selling, upon which this explanation draws, see "Short-Selling: What Is Short-Selling?," http://www.investopedia.com/university/shortselling/shortselling1.asp.

8. Philip Booth, "Short Selling, Imprudence and the Archbishop of York," IEA Blog, October 2, 2008, http://www.iea.org.uk/blog/short-selling-imprudence-and-the-archbishop-of-york.

9. See James Chanos, president, Kynikos Associates, "Prepared Statement," U.S. Securities and Exchange Commission Roundtable on Hedge Funds. Panel discussion: "Hedge Fund Strategies and Market Participation," May 15, 2003, https://www.sec.gov/spotlight/hedgefunds/hedge-chanos.htm.

10. Ibid.

11. Benedict XVI, "Meeting with the Parish Priests and the Clergy of the Diocese of Rome," February 26, 2009, http://www.vatican.va/holy_father/benedict_xvi/speeches/2009/february/documents/hf_ben-xvi_spe_20090226_clergy-rome_en.html.

12. Luis Molina, S.J., *De iustitia et iure*, vol. 2, *Coloniae Allobrogum*, 1759 (originally published Cuenca, 1593/1597), disputation 407, paragraph 7.

13. Raymond de Roover, *Business, Banking, and Economic Thought in Late-Medieval and Early Modern Europe*, ed. Julius Kirshner (Chicago: University of Chicago Press, 1974), 71, 345; and Arrigo Castellani (ed.), *Nuovi testi fiorentini del Dugento* (Florence: Sansoni, 1952), I, 207.

14. Roover, *Business, Banking, and Economic Thought*, 73.

15. See Thomas Divine, S.J., *Interest: An Historical and Analytical Study in Economics and Modern Ethics* (Milwaukee, WI: Marquette University Press, 1959), 44.

16. Ibid., xiii.

17. See John Finnis, *Moral Absolutes: Tradition, Revision, and Truth* (Washington, DC: CUA Press, 1988).

18. Ibid., 111–18.

19. See John Finnis, *Natural Law and Natural Rights* (Oxford: Clarendon Press, 1980), 111–18.

20. James Martin, S.J., "Why the Church Needs Business," *America*, December 19, 2013, http://americamagazine.org/content/all-things/why-church-needs-business.

21. Shawn Tully, "This Pope Means Business," *Fortune*, August 14, 2014, http://fortune.com/2014/08/14/this-pope-means-business.

22. See Wilhelm F. Kasch, "Geld und Glaube: Problemaufriß einer defizitären Beziehung," in Wilhelm F. Kasch, Friedrich Beutter, and Karl Klasen (eds.), *Geld und Glaube* (Paderborn: Schöningh, 1979), 19–70.

23. St. John XXIII, *Mater et magistra* (1961), no. 129, http://www.vatican.va/holy_father/john_xxiii/encyclicals/documents/hf_j-xxiii_enc_15051961_mater_en.html.

24. St. John Paul II, *Centesimus annus* (1991), nos. 19 and 48, http://www.vatican.va/holy_father/john_paul_ii/encyclicals/documents/hf_jp-ii_enc_01051991_centesimus-annus_en.html.

25. See *Compendium of the Social Doctrine of the Church* (2004), nos.368–69, http://www.vatican.va/roman_curia/pontifical_councils/justpeace/documents/rc_pc_justpeace_doc_20060526_compendio-dott-soc_en.html.

26. See Pontifical Council for Justice and Peace, "A New Pact to Reestablish the International Financial System" (2008), http://www.zenit.org/en/articles/vatican-statement-on-doha-meeting.

27. See Pontifical Council for Justice and Peace, *Towards Reforming the International Financial and Monetary Systems in the Context of Global Public Authority* (2011), http://www.vatican.va/roman_curia/pontifical_councils/justpeace/documents/rc_pc_justpeace_doc_20111024_nota_en.html.

28. See, for instance, Samuel Gregg, "Catholics, Finance, and the Perils of Conventional Wisdom," *National Review*, October 24, 2011, http://www.nationalreview.com/corner/281099/catholics-finance-and-perils-conventional-wisdom-samuel-gregg.

29. See Jacques Bichot, "*Sollicitudo rei socialis*: Finances et structures de péché," in Paul D. Dembinski (ed.), *Pratiques financières, regards chrétiens,* (Paris: DDB, 2009), 85.

30. The differences are well explained in Jörg Guido Hülsmann, *The Ethics of Money Production* (Auburn, AL: Ludwig von Mises Institute, 2008), 34–41.

31. See Robert P. George, *In Defense of Natural Law* (Oxford: Oxford University Press, 1999), 108–9.

32. Thomas Aquinas, *Summa theologiae* [hereafter ST] (London: Blackfriars, 1963), I-II, q. 95, a. 2.

33. Alejandro A. Chafuen, *Faith and Liberty: The Economic Thought of the Late Scholastics* (Lanham, MD: Lexington Books, 2003), 58.

34. See Stephen Green, *Good Value: Reflections on Money, Morality, and an Uncertain World* (London: Penguin Books, 2009), 78.

35. Pierre de Lauzun, *Finance: Un regard chrétien* (Paris: Éditions Embrasure, 2013), 207 (my translation).

36. See Francesco D'Acunto, Marcel Prokopczuk, and Michael Weber, "Distrust in Finance Lingers: Jewish Persecution and Household Investment," September 2014, http://faculty.haas.berkeley.edu/francesco_dacunto/papers/AntisemFinW_Jun14.pdf.

2. Detestable to God and Man

1. Dante Alighieri, *The Divine Comedy: Inferno; Purgatorio; Paradiso*, trans. Allen Mandelbaum (New York: Random House, 2013), Canto XI.

2. Tómas de Mercado, *Suma de tratos y contratos*, ed. R. Sierra Bravo (Madrid: IEP, 1975 [1571]), no. 15.

3. See Federal Deposit Insurance Corporation, "Failed Bank List," http://www.fdic.gov/bank/individual/failed/banklist.html.

4. See Daniel Steinvorth, "Holy Bond Loosens: Austerity Creeps Up on Greek Orthodox Church," *Spiegel International*, October 2, 2012, http://www.spiegel.de/international/europe/crisis-prompts-greek-government-to-push-austerity-on-orthodox-church-a-858905.html.

5. See Rodney Stark, *The Rise of Christianity: How the Obscure, Marginal Jesus Movement Became the Dominant Religious Force in the Western World in a Few Centuries* (Princeton: Princeton University Press, 1996).

6. Clement of Alexandria, *Stromata,* vol. 2, *Ante-Nicene Fathers*, ed. Alexander Roberts, James Donaldson, and A. Cleveland Coxe; trans. William Wilson (Buffalo, NY: Christian Literature Publishing, 1885): I, 20.

7. John Kells Ingram, *A History of Political Economy* (London: A&C Black, 1923), 21.

8. See George. J. Costournes, "Development of Banking and Related Bookkeeping Techniques in Ancient Greece, 400–300 B.C., " *International Journal of Accounting* 7, no. 2 (1973): 75–81.

9. See Glyn Davies, *A History of Money: From Ancient Times to the Present Day* (Cardiff: University of Wales, 2002), 74.

10. See, for instance, Raymond Bogaert, *Banques et banquiers dans les cites grecques* (Leyden: A. W. Sitjhoff, 1968), 391–93.

11. Divine, *Interest*, 4.

12. Ibid., 3.

13. See Davies, *History of Money*, 71–73.

14. Plato, *The Republic*, vol. II, books 6–10, trans. Christopher Emlyn-Jones and William Preddy (Loeb Classical Library; Cambridge, MA: Harvard University Press, 2013), bk. VIII, nos. 555c, 555e, 556a.

15. See Aristotle, *Politics*, ed. and trans. Carnes Lord (2nd ed.; Chicago: University of Chicago Press, 2013), I.9.8.

16. See, for example, Aristotle, *On Rhetoric: A Theory of Civic Discourse*, trans. George A. Kennedy (New York: Oxford University Press, 2006), bk. II, chap. 16.

17. Aristotle, *The Nicomachean Ethics*, ed. Hugh Tredennick; trans. J. A. K. Thomson (further rev. ed.; London: Penguin Books, 2003), bk. IV, I, 44.

18. See Aristotle, *Politics*, no. 5.

19. See Lucius Annaeus Seneca, *On Benefits*, trans. Miriam Griffin and Brad Inwood (Chicago: University of Chicago Press, 2010), bk. VII, 10.

20. See Cato and Varra, *On Agriculture*, trans. W. D. Hooper and Harrison Boyd Ash (rev. ed.; Cambridge, MA: Harvard University Press, 1934), bk. I, 1.

21. John T. Noonan, Jr., "Authority, Usury, and Contraception," *Cross Currents* 55 (1966): 57.

22. Thomas Divine, S.J., "Comparatio cum questione de usuris," in John C. Ford, S.J., and Germain Grisez, "Five Briefer Comments in English on 'Schema documenti de responsabili paternitate' Prepared by Dr. Grisez and Five Longer Comments in Latin on '*Relatione Finali*' [that is, 'Rapport Final'] Prepared by Fr. Ford" (1966), 21, www.twotlj.org/F-G-4-Ott-4.pdf.

23. See, for instance, Barbara Newman, "The Passion of the Jews of Prague: The Pogrom of 1389 and the Lessons of a Medieval Parody," *Church History*, 81, no. 1 (March 2012), 1–26.

24. See Rodger Charles, S.J., *Christian Social Witness and Teaching: The Catholic Tradition from Genesis to Centesimus Annus*, vol. 1, *From Biblical Times to the Late Nineteenth Century* (Leominster: Gracewing, 1998), 21.

25. Ibid., 20.

26. Ibid., 21.

27. Divine, "Comparatio cum questione de usuris," 21.

28. Ibid.

29. Ibid.

30. See Urban III, *Decretales*, V, 19, 10, col. 814; see also Aquinas, ST, II-II, q. 78, a. 1.

31. See Clement of Alexandria, *Stromata*, 1.2, c. 18.

32. Basil the Great, "Psalm 14 *Homily* against *Usury,*" 1, http://www.earlychurchtexts.com/public/basil_homily_psalm_14_against_usury.htm.

33. See Divine, *Interest*, 30.

34. See Jerome, *Commentaria in Ezechielem*, 18.5, in J. P. Migne (ed.), *Patrologiae cursus completus: Series latina*, vol. 25 (Paris: Apud Garnier Fratres, 1845), cols. 176–77.

35. Henry Chadwick, *The Cambridge History of Medieval Political Thought* (Cambridge: Cambridge University Press, 1988), 15.

36. St. Gregory of Tours, *The History of the Franks*, ed. Lewis Thorpe (Baltimore: Penguin, 1974), bk. 3, no. 34.

37. See Heinrich Denzinger (ed.), *Compendium of Creeds, Definitions, and Declarations on Matters of Faith and Morals*, rev. Peter Hünermann; ed. (English ed.) Robert Fastiggi and Anne Englund Nash (43rd ed.; San Francisco: Ignatius Press, 2012), 280–81.

38. See Divine, *Interest*, 35.

39. Jules Favre, *Le Prêt à intérêt dans l'ancienne France* (Paris: A. Rousseau, 1900), 51.

40. See John T. Noonan, Jr., *The Scholastic Analysis of Usury* (Cambridge, MA: Harvard University Press, 1957), 17–18.

41. See Robert S. Lopez, *The Commercial Revolution of the Middle Ages 950–1350* (Cambridge: Cambridge University Press, 1976), 23.

42. On the subject of the Byzantine economy, particularly money, banking, and interest, see Cécile Morrison, "Byzantine Money: Its Production and Circulation," in Angeliki E. Laiou (ed.), *The Economic History of Byzantium from the Seventh through the Fifteenth Century* (Washington, DC: Dumbarton Oaks Studies, 2007), III, 909; and Demetrios Gofas, "The Byzantine Law of Interest," in ibid., 1095–1104.

43. See Charles, *Christian Social Witness and Teaching*, I, 31–32.

44. Ibid., 126.

45. Ibid.

46. See Davies, *History of Money*, 97.

47. See ibid., 100–106.

48. See Philip Grierson and M. A. S. Blackburn, *Medieval European Coinage*, vol. 1, *The Early Middle Ages (5th–10th Centuries)* (Cambridge: Cambridge University Press, 1986), 156.

49. See John Gilchrist, *The Church and Economic Activity in the Middle Ages* (New York: Macmillan, 1969), 51.

50. See, for instance, Ricardo Crespo, *A Re-Assessment of Aristotle's Economic Thought* (London: Routledge, 2013).

51. Favre, *Le Prêt à intérêt*, 51.

52. See Sylvain Gouguenheim, *Aristote au Mont Saint-Michel: La racines grecques de l'Europe chrétienne* (Paris: Éditions du Seuil, 2008).

3. *Financial Revolution: Christianity and the Rise of Capital*

1. Quoted in M. Pachant, "St Bernardin de Sienne et l'usure," *Le Moyen Age* 69 (1963): 743ff.

2. Petrus Olivi, *De contractibus usurariis* (Siena: Bibliotec Comunale), cod. U. V. 6, fol. 307.

3. Quoted in Noonan, *Scholastic Analysis*, 74.

4. Bernardine of Siena, *Quadragesimale de evangelio aeterno: Sermones XXVII–LIII* (Florence: Ad Claras Aquas, 1956), Sermo 34:2 (my emphasis).

5. See Edwin S. Hunt and James M. Murray, *A History of Business in Medieval Europe, 1200–1500* (Cambridge: Cambridge University Press, 1999), 216.

6. See Bernard Lazare, *Antisemitism: Its History and Causes* (New York: International Library, 1903), 114–15.

7. See Umberto Benigni, "Montes Pietatis," in *The Catholic Encyclopedia* (New York: Robert Appleton Company, 1911), 534–36.

8. See Noonan, *Scholastic Analysis*, 295.

9. See Benigni, "Montes Pietatis," 534–36.

10. See Monte dei Paschi di Siena, http://english.mps.it.

11. See Martinus Azpilcueta ab Doctor Navarrus, *Enchiridion sive manuale confessaniorum et poenitentium: Tractatus de usuris* (Antwerp: Apud viduam & haeredes Petri Belleri, 1601), 20 nn. 61–62.

12. Joseph Schumpeter, *History of Economic Analysis* (New York: Oxford University Press, 1954), 122.

13. Lopez, *Commercial Revolution*, 31.

14. See Diana Wood, *Medieval Economic Thought* (Cambridge: Cambridge University Press, 2002), 5.

15. Gilchrist, *Church and Economic Activity*, 94f.; and S. B. Clough and R. T. Rapp, *European Economic History* (New York: McGraw-Hill, 1975), 110–20.

16. Randall Collins, *Weberian Sociological Theory* (Cambridge: Cambridge University Press, 1986), 47.

17. See Charles, *Christian Social Witness*, I, 129.

18. Roover, *Business, Banking, and Economic Thought*, 120.

19. See Hunt and Murray, *History of Business*, 62–63.

20. See William N. Goetzmann, "Fibonacci and the Financial Revolution," in William N. Goetzmann and K. Geert Rouwenhorst (eds.), *The Origins of Value: The Financial Innovations That Created Modern Capital Markets* (Oxford: Oxford University Press, 2005), 123–43.

21. See Hunt and Murray, *History of Business*, 60–61.

22. See ibid., 216–17.

23. See Wood, *Medieval Economic Thought*, 79.

24. See Rodney Stark, *How the West Won: The Neglected Story of the Triumph of Modernity* (Wilmington, DE: ISI Books, 2014), 131–32.

25. See Davies, *History of Money*, 155.

26. See, for instance, Léopold Delisle, *Mémoire sur les operations financières des templiers* (Whitefish, MT: Kessinger Publishing, 2010 [1888]).

27. See Lester K. Little, *Religious Poverty and the Profit Economy in Medieval Europe* (Ithaca, NY: Cornell University Press, 1978), 65.

28. See James M. Poterba, "Annuities in Early Modern Europe," in *The Origins of Value: The Financial Innovations That Created Modern Capital Markets*, ed. William N. Goetzmann and K. Geert Rouwenhorst (Oxford: Oxford University Press, 2005), 209.

29. See Hunt and Murray, *History of Business*, 209–12.

30. See Roover, *Business, Banking, and Economic Thought*, 201.

31. See Raymond de Roover, *Money, Banking and Credit in Medieval Bruges—Italian Merchant Bankers, Lombards and Money Changers—A Study in the Origins of Banking* (Cambridge, MA: Medieval Academy of America, 1942), 9–76, 171–98, 247–98.

32. See Abbott Payson Usher, *The Early History of Deposit Banking in Mediterranean Europe* (Cambridge, MA: Harvard University Press, 1943).

33. See Divine, *Interest*, 40.

34. See Henri Pirenne, *Economic and Social History of Medieval Europe* (New York: Harcourt Brace, 1937), 139.

35. See Roover, *Business, Banking, and Economic Thought*, 184.

36. See Charles Kindleberger, *A Financial History of Western Europe* (London: Routledge, 1984), 43.

37. Stark, *How the West Won*, 138.

38. See Aldo de Maddalena and Hermann Kellenbenz (eds.), *La repubblica internazionale del denaro tra XV e XVII secolo* (Bologna: Il Mulino, 1986).

39. See Heinrich Sieveking, *Die Casa di S. Giorgi*, vol. III (Freiburg in Breisgau: Volkswirtschaftliche Abhandlungen, 1899), 44.

40. See Hunt and Murray, *History of Business*, 71.

41. See ibid., 210.

42. See ibid.

43. See Armando Sapori, "La registrazione del libri di commercio in Toscana nell'anno 1605," *Rivista del diretto commercial e del diretto generale delle obbligazionale* 29 (1931): 9–10.

44. Schumpeter, *History of Economic Analysis*, 78.

45. Ibid., 105.

46. Pirenne, *Economic and Social History*, 13.

47. See ibid., 120.

48. Charles, *Christian Social Witness and Teaching*, I, 129.

49. Noonan, *Scholastic Analysis*, 2.

50. Schumpeter, *History of Economic Analysis*, 99.

51. See Odd Langholm, *Economics in the Medieval Schools: Wealth, Exchange, Value, Money and Usury according to the Paris Theological Tradition, 1200–1350* (New York: E. J. Brill, 1992), 77.

52. See Divine, *Interest*, 41.

53. See Gouguenheim, *Aristote au Mont Saint-Michel*, 11–73.

54. See Langholm, *Economics in the Medieval Schools*, 237.

55. See Divine, *Interest*, 41.

56. Cited in Noonan, *Scholastic Analysis*, 182.

57. See Rudolf Sohm, *The Institutes: A Textbook of the History and System of Roman Private Law* (Oxford: Clarendon Press, 1892), 372–73.

58. See Charles, *Christian Social Witness and Teaching*, I, 203.

59. See Thomae de Chobham, *Summa Confessorum*, ed. F. Broomfield (Analecta Mediaevalia Namurcensia 25; Louvain: Éditions Nauwelaerts, 1968), 7, 6, q. 11.

60. See R. H. Helmhotz, *Canon Law and the Law of England* (London, 1987), 326–29.

61. See Lateran III (1179), Canon 25. "We therefore declare that *notorious* usurers should not be admitted to communion of the altar or receive Christian burial if they die in this sin," http://www.papalencyclicals.net/Councils/ecum11.htm.

62. Cited in Noonan, *Scholastic Analysis*, 182.

63. See Langholm, *Economics in the Medieval Schools*, 525.

64. Aristotle, *Ethics* V, v.

65. *Les registres de Grégoire IX*, ed. Albert Fontemoing (Paris: Librarie Thorin et Fils, 1896), 5, 19, 19, col. 816.

66. See Langholm, *Economics in the Medieval Schools*, 311–12.

67. Richard of Middleton, *Super quatuor libros Sententiarum Petri Lombardi* (Brescia, 1591; reprint., Frankfurt-am-Main, 1961), 2, bk. 4, dist. xiv, art. 5, q. 6 (emphasis added).

68. St. Bernadine of Siena, *Sermons*, ed. Nazareno Orlandi; trans. Helen Robins (Siena: Tipograj, 1920), 42, I, 1.

69. Ibid., 41, I, 3.

70. Wood, *Medieval Economic Thought*, 180.

71. This account follows that in John Finnis, *Aquinas: Moral, Political, and Legal Theory* (Oxford: Oxford University Press, 1998), 200–210.

72. See Aquinas, ST, II–II, q. 77 a. 4c.

73. See ibid., II–II, q. 61 a. 4c; and II–II, q. 77 a. 1, a. 4c and ad. 2.

74. See ibid., II–II, q. 77 a. 1.

75. See ibid., II–II, q. 77 a. 2, ad. 2.

76. See ibid., II–II, q. 77 a. 3, ad. 4.

77. See Roover, *Business, Banking, and Economic Thought*, 331.

78. Finnis, *Aquinas*, 205. A good discussion of *interesse* versus usury may be found in Victor Brants, *L'économie politique au Moyen-Âge* (New York: Franklin, 1970), 145–56.

79. Finnis, *Aquinas*, 205.

80. Schumpeter, *History of Economic Analysis*, 103–4.

81. See Divine, *Interest*, 54.

82. See ibid., 55.

83. Gilchrist, *Church and Economic Activity in the Middle Ages*, 69.

84. See Thomas de Chobham, *Summa Confessorum*, 7, 6, q. 11, ch. 7.

85. Gilchrist, *Economic Activity*, 115 (emphasis added).

86. Wood, *Medieval Economic Thought*, 207.

87. Noonan, *Scholastic Analysis*, 173.

88. See Angelus Carletus de Clavasio, *Summa angelica de casibus conscientiae* (Venice: Georgius Arrivabenus, 1492), n. 7.

89. See Noonan, *Scholastic Analysis*, 209.

90. See J. Strieder, *Jacob Fugger: The Rich Banker and Merchant of Augsburg*, trans. M. Hartsough (New York, 1931).

91. Divine, *Interest*, 58.

92. See Noonan, *Scholastic Analysis*, 210.

93. See Thomas de Vio Caietani, *De societate negotiatoria*, in Paul Zammit (ed.), *Scripta philosophica*; *De nominum analogia*; *De conceptu entis* (Rome: apud Institutum "Angelicum," 1934), no. 432.

94. See Wood, *Medieval Economic Thought*, 198.

95. See, for instance, Molina, *De iustitia*, vol. 2, dispn., 348.

96. See E. F. Gay, *American Treasure and the Price Revolution in Spain, 1501–1650* (Cambridge, MA: Harvard University Press, 1934).

97. See Martín de Azpilcueta, "Commentary on the Resolution of Money" (1556), trans. Jeannine Emery, *Journal of Markets & Morality* 7, no. 1 (2004): 171–312, http://www.marketsandmorality.com/index.php/mandm/article/viewFile/453/443.

98. See ibid.

99. Molina, *De iustitia*, vol. 2, 408.3.

100. See Roover, *Business, Banking, and Economic Thought*, 356; and Noonan, *Scholastic Analysis*, 175–92, 311–39.

101. Giovanni Domenico Peri, *Il Negotiante* (Venice, 1638), Part III, cap. xx, 74–75.

102. See Raymond de Roover, *Gresham on Foreign Exchange: An Essay on Early English Mercantilism* (Cambridge, MA: Harvard University Press, 1949), 164.

103. See, for instance, Thomas Wilson, *Discourse on Usury* (New York: Harcourt, 1925 [1572]).

104. See Jordan Ballor, "Wolfgang Musculus on Psalm 15," in Wolfgang Musculus, *On Righteousness, Oaths, and Usury*, trans. Todd M. Rester (Grand Rapids, MI: CLP Academic, 2013), xlvi–xlvii.

105. Divine, "Comparatio cum questione de usuris," 26.

106. See, for instance, Martin Luther, *Werke* (Erlangen, 1938), vol. XXIII, 283–85.

107. See Martin Luther, *Sermon on Usury* (1519), in Hartmann Grisar, *Luther*, trans. E. M. Lamond (London: K. Paul, Trench, Trüber, 1913–17), 78–98.

108. See Maximilian Neumann, *Geschichte des Wuchers in Deutschland* (Halle: Verlag der Buchhandlung des Waisenhauses, 1865), 487.

109. This summary of Calvin's position is derived from Noonan, *Scholastic Analysis*, 365–67.

110. See Divine, *Interest*, 91.

111. Werner Sombart, *The Quintessence of Capitalism: A Study of the History and Psychology of the Modern Business Man*, trans. M. Epstein (New York: Howard Fertig, 1967), 314.

112. See Noonan, *Scholastic Analysis*, 375–82.

113. See ibid., 382–384; Divine, *Interest*, 107–8

114. Noonan, *Scholastic Analysis of Usury*, 399–400.

4. *Caesar's Coin*

1. See Samuel Gregg, *Becoming Europe* (New York: Encounter Books, 2013), 49–50.

2. Geoffrey Ingham, *The Nature of Money* (Cambridge: Policy Press, 2004), 76.

3. See ibid., 181.

4. See Samuel Gregg, "Beyond Sovereignty: Money and Its Future," *Public Discourse*, 5 March 2010. http://www.thepublicdiscourse.com/2010/03/1171.

5. See Jesus Huerta de Soto, *Money, Bank Credit, and Economic Cycles*, trans. Melinda A. Stroup (3rd ed.; Auburn, AL: Ludwig von Mises Institute, 2012), 59–98.

6. See Plato, *Laws*, bk. 4, 716.

7. See Wood, *Medieval Economic Thought*, 91.

8. Thomas Aquinas, *De regimine principum ad regem Cypri* (Turin: Marietti, 1948), II, 14.

9. Thomas Aquinas, *Commentary on the Nicomachean Ethics*, vol. 1 (Chicago: Regnery, 1964), bk. 5, lect. 9, col. 987.

10. See Pirenne, *Economic and Social History*, 107.

11. See ibid., 108–9.

12. See Giles of Rome, *De ecclesiastica potestate*, trans. R. W. Dyson (Woodbridge, 1986), pt. 3, ch. 12.

13. John Day, *Money and Finance in the Age of Merchant Capitalism* (Oxford: Blackwell, 1999), 59–109.

14. See Langholm, *Economics*, 457.

15. See Wood, *Medieval Economic Thought*, 99–100.

16. See Pirenne, *Economic and Social History*, 112.

17. See Davies, *A History of Money*, 230.

18. Wood, *Medieval Economic Thought*, 102.

19. Constantin Fasolt, *Council and Hierarchy: The Political Thought of William Durant the Younger* (Cambridge: Cambridge University Press, 1991), 231.

20. See Nicholas Oresme, *The De moneta of Nicholas Oresme and English Mint Documents* (1355), trans. Charles Johnson (London: Thomas Nelson and Sons, 1956), ch. 17.

21. See ibid., ch. 6.

22. Ibid., ch. 18.

23. Ibid., ch. 25.

24. Ibid., ch. 20.

25. Ibid.

26. Ibid., ch. 21.

27. See J. W. Baldwin, *The Medieval Theories of the Just Price* (Philadelphia: Transactions of the American Philosophical Society, 1959), Appendix A, 80.

28. Juan de Mariana. S.J., "A Treatise on the Alteration of Money," in

Stephen Grabill (ed.), *Sourcebook in Late-Scholastic Monetary Theory* (Lanham, MD: Lexington Books, 2007), ch. 5.

29. Ibid., ch. 3.

30. Ibid., ch. 7.

31. Ibid., ch. 5.

32. Ibid., ch. 3.

33. Ibid, ch. 13.

34. Langholm, *Economics in the Medieval Schools*, 504–5.

35. Ibid., 104.

36. Oresme, *De moneta*, ch. 5

37. Ibid., ch. 6.

38. Ibid., ch. 16.

39. Ibid., chs. 22, 23, 24.

40. Ibid., ch. 18.

41. See Langholm, *Economics in the Medieval Schools*, 457.

42. See Wood, *Medieval Economic Thought*, 107–9.

43. Mariana, "A Treatise on the Alteration of Money," ch. 3.

44. Ibid.

45. Ibid.

46. Ibid.

47. See Luciano Pezzolo, "Bond and Government Debt in Italian City-States, 1250–1650," in William N. Goetzmann and K. Geert Rouwenhorst (eds.), *The Origins of Value: The Financial Innovations That Created Modern Capital Markets* (Oxford: Oxford University Press, 2005), 145–46.

48. See Hunt and Murray, *History of Business*, 209.

49. Ibid., 206.

50. Noonan, *Scholastic Analysis*, 121–22.

51. See Hunt and Murray, *History of Business*, 207.

52. See Richard A. Goldthwaite, *The Economy of Renaissance Florence* (Baltimore: Johns Hopkins University Press, 2009), 244–55.

53. Noonan, *Scholastic Analysis*, 121–22.

54. See Pezzolo, "Bond and Government Debt," 147, 155, 163.

55. See Hunt and Murray, *History of Business*, 207.

56. See Pezzolo, "Bond and Government Debt," 147, 155, 163.

57. See Noonan, *Scholastic Analysis*, 166.

58. See Laurentius de Ridolfis, *Tractatus de usuris et materiae montis*, republished in *Tractatus universi juris* 7, III (Venice, 1583): 5 ad 1 nn. 15–17.

59. See ibid., 7, III: 5, ad 1, n. 17.

60. Wood, *Medieval Economic Thought,* 167–68.

61. See Hunt and Murray, *History of Business,* 92–95, 116.

62. See Goldthwaite, *Economy of Renaissance Florence,* 231.

63. See Hunt and Murray, *History of Business,* 114.

64. Ibid., 92–95, 116.

65. See Goldthwaite, *Economy of Renaissance Florence,* 232–33, 253.

66. Ibid., 236.

67. See Hunt and Murray, *History of Business,* 92–95, 116.

68. Wood, *Medieval Economic Thought,* 167–68.

69. See Goldthwaite, *Economy of Renaissance Florence,* 236–37.

70. Ibid., 236–37.

71. Ibid., 242–43.

72. Ibid., 244–55.

73. Ibid., 244–45

74. See Usher, *Early History of Deposit Banking,* 276, 331.

75. See Goldthwaite, *Economy of Renaissance Florence,* 238–39.

76. Ibid., 230–31.

77. Ibid., 233.

78. See Pirenne, *Economic and Social History,* 25.

79. See Goldthwaite, *Economy of Renaissance Florence,* 238–39.

80. Ibid., 233.

81. Ibid., 234–35.

82. Ibid., 235.

83. Jean-François Berthelot, Pascal-Alexandre Tissot, Alphonse Bérange, *Corpus iuris civilis: Le Digeste, les Institutes, le Code, les Nouvelles,* ed. de Metz (14 vols., 1803–11), Codex, IV, 59, http://www.histoire dudroit.fr/corpus_iuris_civilis.html.

84. *Corpus iuris canonici,* Decr. II, c. xiv, qu. 4, c. 9, http://digital.library. ucla.edu/canonlaw.

85. See Roover, *Business, Banking, and Economic Thought,* 280.

86. See Leonardus Lessius, *De iustitia et iure caeterisque virtutibus cardinalibus,* libri IV (Paris, 1606), lib. 2, cap. 21, dub. 20.

87. Johannes Althusius, *Politica methodice digesta,* ed. Carl Friedrich (Cambridge, MA: Harvard University Press 1932), ch. XXXII.

88. Lauzun, *Finance: Un regard chrétien,* 115.

89. Benedict XVI, "Meeting with the Representatives of British Society," Westminster Hall, September 17, 2010, http://www.vatican.va/holy_father/benedict_xvi/speeches/2010/september/documents/hf_ben-xvi _spe_20100917_societa-civile_en.html.

5. *Freedom, Flourishing, and Justice*

1. Francis, "Palm Sunday Homily," March 24, 2013, 3, http://www.vatican.va/holy_father/francesco/homilies/2013/documents/papa-francesco_20130324_palme_en.html.

2. Pontifical Council for Justice and Peace, *Towards Reforming*, "Presumption."

3. See also Matt. 11:30; John 8:36; Rom. 8:1; 1 Cor. 7:22.

4. St. Augustine, *The City of God against the Pagans*, trans. R. W. Dyson (New York: Cambridge University Press, 1998), bk. IV, ch. 3.

5. See Finnis, *Moral Absolutes*, 6; and P. Grelot, *Problèmes de morale fondamentale: Un éclairage biblique* (Paris: Éditions du Cerf, 1982), 117.

6. This draws on Samuel Gregg, *On Ordered Liberty* (Lanham, MD: Lexington Books, 2003), 29–50.

7. St. Thomas Aquinas, *Quaestiones disputatae de veritate a quaestione II ad quaestionem IV,* ed. Roberto Busa, S.J. (Rome: Textum Leoninum, 1970), q. 8, a. 6c.

8. Benedict XVI, "10 Commandments Are Sign of God's Love for Us," *Zenit*, September 10, 2012, http://www.zenit.org/article-35488?l=english (my emphasis).

9. Second Vatican Council, Pastoral Constitution on the Church in the Modern World, *Gaudium et Spes* [hereafter GS] (1965), no. 74, http://www.vatican.va/archive/hist_councils/ii_vatican_council/documents/vat-ii_const_19651207_gaudium-et-spes_en.html.

10. Charles Chaput, "Law and Morality in Public Discourse: How Christians Can Rebuild Our Culture," *Public Discourse*, August 7, 2014, http://www.thepublicdiscourse.com/2014/08/13612.

11. See Gregg, *On Ordered Liberty*, 29–50.

12. See Germain Grisez, *The Way of the Lord Jesus*, vol. 2, *Living a Christian Life* (Quincy, IL: Franciscan Press, 1993), 790.

13. See Aquinas, ST, II-II, q. 66 a. 2.

14. Ibid., II-II, q. 66, a. 7.

15. Ibid., II-II, q. 32, a. 5.

16. Domingo de Soto, O.P., *De iustitia et iure* (Madrid: IEP, 1968), bk. 4, q. 3, fol. 105–6.

17. Mercado, *Summa de tractos y contractos*, bk. 2, ch. 2, fol. 19.

18. Juan de Mariana, S.J., *Discurso de las Cosas de la Compãnia* (Biblioteca de Autores Espanoles 31; Madrid: Editions Atlas, 1950), 604.

19. See Samuel Gregg, *Challenging the Modern World: Karol Wojtyla/ John Paul II and the Development of Catholic Social Teaching* (Lanham, MD: Lexington Books, 2002), 40–45.

20. See Frank J. Hanna, *What Your Money Means* (New York: Crossroad Publishing Company, 2008), 23–47.

21. Ibid., 49.

22. St. John Paul II, Encyclical Letter *Sollicitudo rei socialis* [hereafter SRS] (1987), no. 36, http://www.vatican.va/holy_father/john_paul_ii/ encyclicals/documents/hf_jp-ii_enc_30121987_sollicitudo-rei-socialis_ en.html.

23. St. John Paul II, Apostolic Exhortation *Reconciliatio et paenitentia* [hereafter RP] (1984), no. 16, http://www.vatican.va/holy_father/john_ paul_ii/apost_exhortations/documents/hf_jp-ii_exh_02121984_reconcilia- tio-et-paenitentia_en.html.

24. RP, no. 16.

25. SRS, no. 36.

26. *Catechism of the Catholic Church* [hereafter CCC] (1992), nos. 2402–6, http://www.vatican.va/archive/ENG0015/_INDEX.HTM.

27. CCC, nos. 2408–9.

28. CCC, no. 2411.

29. Ibid.

30. Finnis, *Natural Law*, 188.

31. See F. H. Lawson and Bernard Rudden, *Law of Property* (3rd ed.; Oxford: Oxford University Press, 2002), 139.

32. Ibid., 169.

33. For legal recognition of this, see *Re. Wilson, ex parte Vine* (1878) 8 Ch. D. 364, 366.

34. This account follows closely that outlined in Finnis, *Natural Law*, 190–91.

35. CCC, no. 2411.

36. See Aquinas, ST, II-II, q. 58, a. 6c.

37. See Samuel Gregg, "What Is Social Justice?," *Library of Law and Liberty*, April 1, 2013, http://www.libertylawsite.org/liberty-forum/what- is-social-justice; and Paul-Dominique Dognin, O.P., "La notion thomiste de justice face aux exigences modernes," *Revue des sciences philosophiques et théologiques* 45 (1961): 601–40.

6. Understanding Capital, Civilizing Capital

1. See R. Mshana, "The Current Financial System" (January 2004), http://www.oikoumene.org/en/resources/documents/wcc-programmes/public-witness-addressing-poweraffirming-peace/poverty-wealth-and-ecology/finance-speculation-debt/r-mshana-on-current-financial-system.

2. CCC, no. 2409.

3. Oswald Nell-Breuning, S.J., *Grundzüge der Börsenmoral* (Hamburg: Lit Verlag, 1928), 127.

4. Stephen Nakrosis, "The Ethics of Speculation in the Works of Oswald von Nell-Breuning," *Catholic Social Science Review* 18 (2013): 169.

5. See Johannes Messner, *Social Ethics: Natural Law in the Western World*, trans. J. Doherty (St. Louis, MO: Herder & Herder, 1965), 879.

6. Ibid., 876.

7. See Yilmaz Akyüz and Andrew Cornford, "Repaying Debt in the Wake of an International Financial Crisis," *Finance & bien commun*, Supplement no. 2, May 2002, 102.

8. Thomas Friedman, *The Lexus and the Olive Tree: Understanding Globalization* (New York: Macmillan, 2000), 165.

9. See A. de Salins and F. Villeroy de Galhau, *Le développement moderne des activités financières au regard des exigences éthiques du Christianisme* (Vatican City: Conseil Pontifical "Justice et Paix," 1994), 20.

10. Ibid., 25.

11. Benedict XVI, "Address to Participants in the 37th Conference of the FAO," July 1, 2011, http://www.vatican.va/holy_father/benedict_xvi/speeches/2011/july/documents/hf_ben-xvi_spe_20110701_fao_en.html.

12. Francis, "Address to the Participants in the Conference Promoted by the Pontifical Council for Justice and Peace on 'Impact Investing for the Poor,'" June 16, 2014, http://w2.vatican.va/content/francesco/en/speeches/2014/june/documents/papa-francesco_20140616_convegno-justpeace.html.

13. See, for instance, Craig Pirrong, "No Theory? No Evidence? No Problem!," *Regulation* 33, no. 2 (2010): 40.

14. See, for instance, ibid., 38–44.

15. Paul Blustein, *And the Money Kept Rolling In (and Out): Wall Street, the IMF, and the Bankrupting of Argentina* (New York: Public Affairs, 2005), 6.

16. See, for instance, Christopher Matthews, "LIBOR Scandal: Yep, It's as Bad as We Thought," *Time Magazine*, 20 December 2012.

17. See Carrick Mollenkamp, "Bankers Cast Doubt on Key Rate amid Crisis," *Wall Street Journal*, April 16, 2008, http://online.wsj.com/news/articles/SB120831164167818299?mg=reno64-wsj; and Carrick Mollenkamp and Mark Whitehouse, "Study Casts Doubt on Key Rate," *Wall Street Journal*, May 29, 2008, http://online.wsj.com/articles/SB121200703762027135.

18. The scandal is most fully detailed in HM Treasury, "The Wheatley Review of LIBOR: Final Report," September 2012, https://www.gov.uk/government/uploads/system/uploads/attachment_data/file/191762/wheatley_review_libor_finalreport_280912.pdf.

19. See Mollenkamp, "Bankers Cast Doubt on Key Rate."

20. See Lauzun, *Finance*, 178.

21. Ibid., 179.

22. See Roger Lowenstein, *When Genius Failed: The Rise and Fall of Long-Term Capital Management* (New York: Random House, 2000).

23. See Niall Ferguson, *The Ascent of Money* (New York: Penguin, 2008), 346.

24. Benedict XVI, "Letter to the Right Honourable Gordon Brown on the Vigil of the G20 Summit in London" (2009), http://www.vatican.va/holy_father/benedict_xvi/letters/2009/documents/hf_ben-xvi_let_20090330_gordon-brown_en.html.

25. See Benedict XVI, "World Day of Peace Message," January 1, 2009, http://www.vatican.va/holy_father/benedict_xvi/messages/peace/documents/hf_ben-xvi_mes_20081208_xlii-world-day-peace_en.html.

26. Lauzun, *Finance*, 98.

27. See Brian Griffiths, "Ethical Dimensions of Finance," in Martin Schlag and Juan Andrés Mercado (eds.), *Free Markets and the Culture of the Common Good* (London: Springer, 2012), 148.

28. Cited in Philip Booth, "Catholic Social Teaching and the Financial Crash," in *Catholic Social Teaching and the Market Economy*, ed. Philip Booth (London: IEA, 2014), 392.

29. See, for example, Gwen Robinson, "Bonus Supertax Failed, Says Darling," *Financial Times*, September 2, 2010, http://ftalphaville.ft.com/2010/09/02/332351/bonus-supertax-failed-says-darling.

30. David Campbell and Stephen Griffith, "Enron and the End of Corporate Governance," in *Global Governance and the Quest for Justice*, ed. S. Macleod (Oxford: Hart Publishing, 2006), 59.

31. Adam Smith, *An Inquiry into the Nature and Cause of the Wealth of Nations* (Indianapolis: Liberty Fund, 1981 [1776]), 741.

32. See, for instance, the essays in Philip Booth (ed.), *Verdict on the Crash: Causes and Policy Implications* (London: IEA, 2009).

33. See Griffiths, "Ethical Dimensions of Finance," 141.

7. *The Common Good, the State, and Public Finance*

1. Mariana, "A Treatise," ch. 1.

2. St. Augustine, *City of God*, IV, 4.

3. See Allard Dembe and Leslie Boden, "Moral Hazard: A Question of Morality?," *New Solutions: A Journal of Environmental and Occupational Health Policy* 10, no. 3 (2000): 257–79.

4. See Paul Krugman, *The Return of Depression Economics and the Crisis of 2008* (New York: W. W. Norton, 2008), 137.

5. Vernon L. Smith, "The Clinton Housing Bubble," *Wall Street Journal*, December 18, 2007, http://online.wsj.com/articles/SB1197940 91743935595.

6. See Salins and Villeroy de Galhau, *Le développement moderne*, 24.

7. See, for example, Timothy Geithner, *Stress Test* (New York: Crown Publishers, 2014).

8. This is drawn from Roger Koppl, *From Crisis to Confidence* (London: IEA, 2014), 8–9. One can listen to these particular recordings at http://www.rte.ie/news/player/2013/0624/3552597-excerpt-from-anglo-tapes. The full recordings may be found at http://www.independent.ie/blog/listen-to-more-of-the-anglo-recordings-clips-1-to-9-29382473.html .

9. "Two Anglo Executives Deny Misleading Central Bank over Funding," *RTE News*, June 24, 2013, http://www.rte.ie/news/business/2013/0624/458433-anglo-central-bank.

10. Koppl, *From Crisis to Confidence*, 9–10.

11. Florian Hett and Alexander Schmidt, "Do Bank Bail-Outs Create Moral Hazard? Evidence from the Recent Financial Crisis," March 1, 2012, 2, http://www.iwh-halle.de/d/start/news/workshops/20120524/pdf/hett.pdf.

12. Ibid., 2.

13. Ibid., 25.

14. Cited in John Carney, "Anna Schwartz Says the Bailouts Leave the Market 'Bewildered'" (2009), http://www.businessinsider.com/anna-schwartz-says-the-bailouts-leave-the-market-bewildered-2009-6.

15. For a variety of views on this subject, see Julie Creswell and Ben White, "The Guys from 'Government Sachs,'" *New York Times*, October 17, 2008, http://www.nytimes.com/2008/10/19/business/19gold.html?_r=4&scp=1&sq=%22government%20sachs%22&st=cse&.

16. Archbishop Rowan Williams, "Patience and Trust: The New Economic Foundations," *The Guardian*, March 8, 2009, http://www.theguardian.com/world/2009/mar/09/rowan-williams-lecture-full-text.

17. This draws in part on James Kwak, "Regulatory Capital Arbitrage for Beginners" (2009), http://baselinescenario.com/2009/05/30/regulatory-capital-arbitrage-for-beginners.

18. See "War on Wonga: We're Putting You Out of Business, Archbishop of Canterbury Justin Welby Tells Payday Loans Company," *The Independent*, July 25, 2013, http://www.independent.co.uk/news/uk/home-news/war-on-wonga-were-putting-you-out-of-business-archbishop-of-canterbury-justin-welby-tells-payday-loans-company-8730839.html.

19. Booth, "Catholic Social Teaching and the Financial Crash," 396.

20. Ibid.

21. Peter Wallison, "Four Years of Dodd-Frank Damage," *Wall Street Journal*, July 20, 2014, http://online.wsj.com/articles/peter-wallison-four-years-of-dodd-frank-damage-1405893333.

22. Green, *Good Value*, 132.

23. Bishops' Conference of England and Wales, *Choosing the Common Good* (Stoke in Trent: Alive Publishing, 2010), 10.

24. Ibid., 9–10.

25. Ibid.

26. This is detailed in Thomas A. Durkin, Gregory Elliehausen, Michael E. Staten, and Todd J. Zywicki, *Consumer Credit and the American Economy* (Oxford: Oxford University Press, 2014).

27. Bishops' Conference of England and Wales, *Choosing the Common Good*, 12.

28. Messner, *Social Ethics*, 777.

29. See Oresme, *De moneta*, ch. 1.

30. See Sean Fieler, "Easy Money Is Punishing the Middle Class," *Wall Street Journal*, September 26, 2012, http://online.wsj.com/articles/SB10000872396390444180004578016200287341688.

31. For such a case with regard to quantitative easing, see Charles Clark, "The Ethics of Quantitative Easing: A Catholic Perspective," *Cardus*, November 28, 2011, http://www.cardus.ca/comment/article/2999/the-ethics-of-quantitative-easing-a-catholic-perspective/cardus.ca. For an

opposing view, see Jonathan Wellum, "The 'Occupy' Debt Serfs," *Cardus*, November 28, 2011, http://www.cardus.ca/comment/article/3000/the-occupy-debt-serfs.

32. See Messner, *Social Ethics*, 774–75.

33. Hülsmann, *Ethics of Money Production*, 100.

34. Ruchir Sharma, "Liberals Love the 'One Percent,'" *Wall Street Journal*, July 29, 2014, http://online.wsj.com/articles/ruchir-sharma-liberals-the-one-percent-1406676743?mod=Opinion_newsreel_2.

35. Williams, "Patience and Trust."

36. Pontifical Council for Justice and Peace, *Towards Reforming the International Financial and Monetary System*, Section 4.

37. See, for example, Benedict XVI, *Caritas in veritate* (2009), no. 67.

38. Pontifical Council for Justice and Peace, *Towards Reforming the International Financial and Monetary System*, Section 3.

39. Friedrich A. Hayek, The Pretense of Knowledge, Lecture to the Memory of Alfred Nobel, December 11, 1974, http://www.nobelprize.org/nobel_prizes/economic-sciences/laureates/1974/hayek-lecture.html.

8. *Finance as* Vocatio, *Finance as* Magnificentia

1. Horace, *Odes*, IV, 9, 1. 45.

2. QA, no. 51 (emphasis added).

3. Francis, Apostolic Exhortation *Evangelii gaudium* [hereafter EG] (2013), no. 203, http://w2.vatican.va/content/francesco/en/apost_exhortations/documents/papa-francesco_esortazione-ap_20131124_evangelii-gaudium.html.

4. See Brian Griffiths, *The Creation of Wealth* (London: Hodder & Stoughton, 1984).

5. Thomas Aquinas, *De regimine principum ad regem Cypri* (Turin: Marietti, 1948), I, 6.

6. See J. W. O'Malley, *The First Jesuits* (Cambridge, MA: Harvard University Press, 1995).

7. Alister E. McGrath, "Calvin and the Christian Calling," *First Things* 94 (June/July 1999): 31–35.

8. See Robert S. Michaelson, "Changes in the Puritan Concept of Calling or Vocation," *The New England Quarterly* 26, no. 3 (1953): 315–36.

9. See D. Kelly, *The Westminster Confession of Faith: An Authentic Modern Version* (New York: Summertown Texts, 1992).

10. Thomas Hopko, "Finding One's Vocation in Life," in *Orthodox*

Church in America Resource Handbook (1996), http://oca.org/resource-handbook/theology/finding-ones-vocation-in-life.

11. Josemaría Escrivá, "The Christian Vocation," December 2, 1951, http://www.josemariaescriva.info/docs/the-christian-vocation.pdf.

12. CCC, no. 2392.

13. EG, no. 53.

14. Hanna, *What Your Money Means*, 110.

15. Ibid.

16. Ambrose, *Decretals*, Dist. xlvii, can. Sicut, ii.

17. Anthony G. Percy, *Entrepreneurship in the Catholic Tradition* (Lanham, MD: Lexington Books, 2010), 73.

18. Green, *Good Value*, 155.

19. Vincent A. Yzermans (ed.), *The Unwearied Advocate: Public Addresses of His Holiness Pope Pius XII* (St. Cloud: Vincent A. Yzermans, 1954), 79.

20. Percy, *Entrepreneurship in the Catholic Tradition*, 107.

21. Yzermans, *The Unwearied Advocate*, III, 80.

22. Pope Pius XII, "Function of Bankers," *The Catholic Mind* 52, no. 1094 (1951): 121.

23. Ibid., 122.

24. Ibid.

25. Ibid., 121.

26. Philip Booth, "The Poorest Will Suffer if We Ignore the Real Evidence on Payday Loans," *City AM*, December 11, 2012, http://www.cityam.com/article/poorest-will-suffer-if-we-ignore-real-evidence-payday-loans.

27. Ibid.

28. See Samuel Gregg, "Bankers and Processors Are Not Moral Police," *American Banker*, October 15, 2013, http://www.americanbanker.com/bankthink/bankers-and-processors-are-not-moral-police-1062818-1.html.

29. Benedict XVI, *Light of the World* (San Francisco: Ignatius Press, 2010), 47.

30. Ibid.

31. Hülsmann, *Ethics of Money Production*, 220.

32. Ibid.

33. Ibid., 221.

34. See Griffiths, "Ethical Dimensions of Finance," 144–45.

35. Cited in Margaret Ackrill and Leslie Hannah, *Barclays: The Business of Banking, 1690–1996* (Cambridge: Cambridge University Press, 2001), 46.

36. Adam Smith, *The Theory of Moral Sentiments* (6th ed.; Indianapolis: Liberty Fund, 1982 [1790]), VI.ii.3.3.

37. Ibid., VI.ii.3.4.

38. See Ryan Patrick Hanley, *Adam Smith and the Character of Virtue* (Cambridge: Cambridge University Press, 2009), 187–202.

39. Aquinas, ST, II-II, q. 134, a. 3.

40. Ibid., q. 134, a. 1.

41. Ibid., q. 134, a. 4 (emphasis added).

42. See ibid., q. 134, a. 3.

43. James D. Bratt (ed.), *Abraham Kuyper, A Centennial Reader* (Grand Rapids: Wm. B. Eerdmans, 1998), 488.

Index

Acknowledgments

Any conversation that involves religion and money is never likely to be an easy one. Yet in a globalized world and economy in which capital is being put to ever more creative and faster uses, it is a topic that is only likely to increase in significance—especially in a world that, outside parts of Western Europe and certain regions of North America, is growing more religious.

Fortunately, I have had a good number of friends and colleagues with whom I have been able to have constructive conversations about the world of banking, finance, and capital and the ways in which Jewish and Christian traditions and thinkers have addressed the manifold issues associated with this subject.

The list is long but it includes the late Whitney Ball, Jordan Ballor, Philip Booth, the late Father Rodger Charles, S.J., Sean Fieler, Declan Ganley, David Goldman, Lord Griffiths of Fforestfach, Steven Grosby, Frank Hanna III, Ian Harper, Sir Michael Hintze, Kishore Jayabalan, Bishop Kęstutis Kėvalas, Ambassador John McCarthy QC, Father C. J. McCloskey, Heinrich Liechtenstein, Rabbi Isaac Lifshitz, Michael Matheson Miller, Kris Alan Mauren, Michael Novak, Gerald O'Driscoll, Dylan Pahman, Catherine Pakaluk, Father Martin Rhonheimer, Jay W. Richards, Carroll Ríos de Rodríguez, Father Martin Schlag, Father Robert A. Sirico, Vernon Smith, Manfred Spieker, James R. Stoner, Joseph Swanson, Maximilian B. Torres, Andreas Widmer, and Christof Zellenberg.

Many thanks are also due to the publishers of this book, especially Gwendolin Herder and John Zmirak.

Finally, I want to single out two particular individuals. The first is Elena Leontjeva. Her interest in this topic is untiring, as has been her relentless encouragement to write this book. The second is His

Eminence George Cardinal Pell for agreeing to write the Foreword, despite his heavy responsibilities as the Catholic Church's inaugural Prefect for the Secretariat of the Economy.

The usual caveats about errors and mistakes apply.

About the Author

Samuel Gregg is research director at the Acton Institute. He writes and speaks regularly on morality and economics. He is the author of many books, including, among others, *On Ordered Liberty* (2003), *The Modern Papacy* (2009), *Wilhelm Röpke's Political Economy* (2010), *Becoming Europe* (2013), and his prize-winning *The Commercial Society* (2006).

He is published in journals such as the *Harvard Journal of Law and Public Policy*; *Journal of Markets & Morality*; *Economic Affairs*; *Notre Dame Journal of Law, Ethics and Public Policy*; *Library of Law and Liberty*; *First Things*; *Ave Maria Law Review*; *Oxford Analytica*; *Communio*; *Journal of Scottish Philosophy*; *University Bookman*; *Foreign Affairs*; and *Policy*. His opinion pieces have appeared in the *Wall Street Journal Europe*; *American Banker*; *Investors Business Daily*; *National Review*; *Public Discourse*; *American Spectator*; *The Federalist*; *Australian Financial Review*; and *Business Review Weekly*. He holds an MA in political philosophy from the University of Melbourne, and a Doctor of Philosophy degree in moral philosophy and political economy from the University of Oxford.

About the Publisher

The CROSSROAD PUBLISHING COMPANY publishes CROSSROAD and HERDER & HERDER books. We offer a 200-year global family tradition of books on spiritual living and religious thought. We promote reading as a time-tested discipline for focus and understanding. We help authors shape, clarify, write, and effectively promote their ideas. We select, edit, and distribute books. With our expertise and passion we provide wholesome spiritual nourishment for heart, mind, and soul through the written word.

Other Books We Thought You Might Like

Samuel Gregg
TEA PARTY CATHOLIC
The Catholic Case for Limited Government,
a Free Economy, and Human Flourishing
978-0-8245-4981-7, pb, 272 pages

What is a Catholic to make of the American love for liberty? A deep look at American freedom shows a much more profound agreement than most Americans or Catholics recognize.

"The book is as carefully and, indeed, rigorously argued as it is provocatively titled. It is a great resource for anyone—Catholic or not—who wants to know what the Church really teaches about the moral requirement of the socio-economic and political orders." — Prof. Robert George, Princeton University

"A stimulating reading of Catholic social teaching and the American founding and its application to some of today's most sharply contested public policy issues, particularly those touching on economic and religious freedom." — George Weigel, papal biographer and author of *Evangelical Catholicism*

Support your local bookstore or order
directly from the publisher at
www.CrossroadPublishing.com

To request a catalog or inquire about
quantity orders, please e-mail
sales@CrossroadPublishing.com

The Crossroad Publishing Company

Related Reading

Robert Royal
THE CATHOLIC MARTYRS
OF THE TWENTIETH CENTURY
A Comprehensive World History
978-0-8245-2414-2, pb, 430 pages

From the Catholic martyrs at Auschwitz to Oscar Romero;
from Ita Ford and her companions to the recent murders
of Christians in India: it is estimated that more than one
million believers died for their faith in the "century of
progress" we have just experienced.

In *The Catholic Martyrs of the Twentieth Century*, Robert
Royal presents a wide-ranging history of these martyrs.
The book traces the specific situation of each area and time
when martyrdom occurred, and studies the political system
and the reason for confrontation.

Support your local bookstore or order
directly from the publisher at
www.CrossroadPublishing.com

To request a catalog or inquire about
quantity orders, please e-mail
sales@CrossroadPublishing.com

The Crossroad Publishing Company

The Pope Francis Resource Library

Diego Fares,
Foreword by Antonio Spadaro, SJ
THE HEART OF POPE FRANCIS
How a New Culture of Encounter Is Changing
the Church and the World
978-0-8245-2074-8, $14.95 hc, 100 pages

A presentation of what lies at the heart of Pope Francis's
pontificate: a keen interest in people and a passion for
understanding the life experience of others. Written by his
long-time friend and fellow Jesuit, this book clarifies the
underlying thoughts and choices Jorge Bergoglio has made
throughout his life in developing a culture of encounter
that he now proposes as the basis for the rebirth of the
whole church, and the world.

Support your local bookstore or order
directly from the publisher at
www.CrossroadPublishing.com

To request a catalog or inquire about
quantity orders, please e-mail
sales@CrossroadPublishing.com

The Crossroad Publishing Company